THE OBSERVER'S BOOK OF
COMMON INSECTS AND SPIDERS

The Observer's Books

THE OBSERVER'S BOOK OF

COMMON
INSECTS
AND SPIDERS

By
E. F. LINSSEN, F.Z.S., F.R.E.S.

*With Sections on Trichoptera
and Lepidoptera by*
L. HUGH NEWMAN, F.R.E.S., F.R.H.S.

*Outlining
ALL THE BRITISH ORDERS
with 64 Plates, 32 of which are in colour,
comprising 323 figures*

Linda Norris

FREDERICK WARNE & CO. LTD.
FREDERICK WARNE & CO. INC.
LONDON · NEW YORK

PREFACE

EVERY INSECT order found in the British Isles is outlined in this pocket-book, and illustrations are given of many of the more common species. No book can, however, in any manner deal adequately with the whole of our insect fauna, of which we have over 20,000 species, and consequently writers can give only a generalized picture of insects made up from a few selected examples of species which the nature lover may find during his countryside rambles.

Because of the dependence of spiders on insects for food, and in deference to a custom of including them in popular books, they have been included in this volume—notwithstanding the fact that they belong to an entirely separate class of animals.

The main part of this book has been written by E. F. Linssen, F.Z.S., F.R.E.S., and the sections dealing with Trichoptera and Lepidoptera by L. Hugh Newman, F.R.E.S., F.R.H.S.

All the photographs reproduced in this book are by E. F. Linssen, with the exception of those appearing on Plates 17 (by E. Botting), 42 (*left*, by D. A. Ashwell ; *right*, by E. A. Robins), 44 and 56 (the upper and lower ones respectively by S. C. Bisserôt) and 63 (R. W. J. Norton).

The colour plates and the rest of the monochrome plates have been prepared by L. G. Goodwin and A. F. Stuart.

CONTENTS

INTRODUCTION

It is not known how many species of insects there are in the world. Well over 700,000 have been scientifically described, however, and it is thought that there must be at least five times as many, an estimate which is probably very conservative. There are at least eight insect species to every one of all other animals put together, and there are over 20,000 kinds of British insects, a most respectable number for an island having a mild temperate climate. The number of insect species thus outnumbers in a most prodigious manner every other kind of life known, whether it be animal or plant.

Insects are to be found everywhere. They live on plants and animals, or inside them. They are to be found in the air, in the earth, and in water. Some of them are as small as one-celled microscopical protozoa, and others are larger than some vertebrates. In the struggle for food they are man's undoubted and constant rivals, and they would defeat his proud dominion on earth were it not that they themselves are held in check by predators and parasites of their own kind. Only they themselves could do this.

As to the numbers of individuals—this is evidently an impossible thing to guess at, but even so the latest estimate, using highly evolved scientific methods, gives the present population of one acre of certain farmland in England as from seven hundred to eight hundred million! An equal number of mites (of the class Arachnida) was found to be present too!

What strikes us most about insects must surely be their energy, especially the persistence with which they apply it; nothing like this is to be found anywhere else in the animal kingdom. The pestering fly in sunshine and the blood-seeking mosquito at night are examples known to us all. The industry of the ant and the bee is another form of it, but in this instance man's admiration is aroused, and renowned philosophical writers like Maeterlinck derived inspiration from examples of virtues to be found among insects. Untiring labour, care of progeny, foresight, fidelity to the community, and the supreme self-sacrifice of the individual for the common good, are indeed qualities which we see exercised by many insects, especially by most bees, wasps, ants and, in warmer climates, termites. But to the entomologist of today such persistence of energy seems all too intimately bound up with an inability to profit from experience. Insects do not learn; they have no individuality. We need but know the peculiarities of a species to predict how its members will react to given conditions.

The behaviour of insects is governed by instinct. In the British Isles this may be seen developed in its highest form in ants, bees and wasps. Behaviour due to instinct is not learned, but is an inherited capacity, although it may be improved by practice. The mysterious force of instinct is shown by the classic example of the Hive Bee, which on leaving the hive for the first time performs all the duties of an expert forager, as if it were a routine performance already done on numerous occasions. Strict routine behaviour is, however, peculiar to instinct, and is always associated with definite situations and occurrences at critical stages of an insect's life, as, for example, when the moment of pupation arrives, or when a Dragonfly nymph climbs out of the water for the first time in its life in order that the fully developed Dragonfly will be able to emerge in its own

8

element, air, which is entirely foreign to the earlier stages of its life.

The quality of our thoughts and actions is due to our acquired experience and the processes of our brain. An insect has a brain, but it is not a true centralized nerve-centre, as in the higher animals. An insect's nervous system consists of a double cord of nerve running along the whole lower length of the body. There are swellings (*ganglia*) at intervals, from which branches of nerves lead into the body-segments. These ganglia have much independence of function and can act as local brains. It is significant that those which command important parts of the body are correspondingly larger in size ; for instance, the thorax bears the legs and wings, and its ganglia are larger than those of the abdomen.

Facts such as these have therefore to be borne in mind when we would advance explanations based on analogy between our own behaviour and what causes it, and the phenomena of a similar kind which we may observe in insects. Such interpretations could easily lead us into complete error. However, although an insect is the puppet of the all-powerful instinct that dominates its life, this does not necessarily make it a mere automaton. If an insect is driven on by instinct and energy, we shall nevertheless perceive that occasionally there is present an awareness of situations, especially in the more evolved species, which indicates some vague mental process which is able to exercise some learning, judgement and control.

It is interesting at this stage, before proceeding further, to compare the conclusions of a present-day naturalist, R. W. G. Hingston, with the reflections of another, the poet Brooke, written at the beginning of the last century. " Every animal, Man included, possesses two sets of mental activity : the one instinctive, automatic, innate ; the other intelligent, plastic and acquired. These two activities are always blended. They may differ immensely in degrees of development, but they never completely separate from each other. The insect mind and the human mind differ mainly in the development of these two factors. . . . The Insect, though predominantly instinctive, possesses also glimmerings of reason." * The poet tells of the structural wonders found in insects, and he does this in a way that is becoming all too rare :—

> " Though numberless these insect tribes of air,
> Though numberless each tribe and species fair,
> Who wing the noon, and brighten in the blaze,
> Innumerous as the sands which bend the seas ;
> These have their organs, arts, and arms, and tools,
> And functions exercised by various rules ;
> The saw, the auger, trowel, piercer, drill ;
> The neat alembic, and nectareous still :
> Their peaceful hours the loom and distaff know :
> But war, the force and fury of the foe,
> The spear, the falchion, and the martial mail,
> And artful stratagem, where strength may fail,
> Each tribe peculiar occupations claim,
> Peculiar beauties deck each wavering frame."

Neither of these authors exaggerates what may be observed and studied in insects.

EXTERNAL STRUCTURE

When we look at an insect, say a beetle, we first notice its hard, characteristic " skin ". This is composed of *chitin*, and forms a shell or case of armour-plating, at the same time fulfilling the important function of a skeleton—an external one,

* From *Problems of Instinct and Intelligence*, by R. W. G. Hingston (Edward Arnold & Co.).

hence called an *exoskeleton*. All muscles are attached to the exoskeleton and support the internal organs of the insect, which are soft. A "set" museum or cabinet specimen is hollow, everything within having dried up. The chitin of the exoskeleton is one of the most effectual of time-resisting materials known, and its indestructible nature, and the forms and colours with which it may be associated, are what have made entomology so particularly fascinating to collectors. This is especially so because it permits the arranging of attractive and permanent collections, which at the same time can be directly correlated with the enthralling life-histories of the insects and details of their behaviour.

The nature of the exoskeleton and the method of breathing put a limit on the maximum size attainable by insects, but even so some exotic species of the order Orthoptera exceed 260 mm. (10¼ in.) in length. Our largest native species are from the order Coleoptera—*Hydrophilus piceus*, the Great Silver Water-beetle, which attains a body length of 48 mm. (1⅞ in.) and *Lucanus cervus*, the Stag Beetle, which may attain 50 mm. (2 in.), while the Emperor Dragonfly (*Anax imperator*) among the order Odonata achieves 75 mm. (3 in.) in length.

The class Insecta is sometimes called the "Hexapoda" ("the six-legged"), indicating an anatomical characteristic constituting a marked morphological difference from other Arthropods. An insect's body has three distinct divisions (see the illustration on page 12), the **head, thorax** (chest) and **abdomen.** The head bears one pair of *antennae* ("feelers" or "horns"), which are sensory in function. The *mouth-parts* are complicated in structure and vary much in the different insect orders, and also frequently at different periods of an insect's life. The thorax bears the

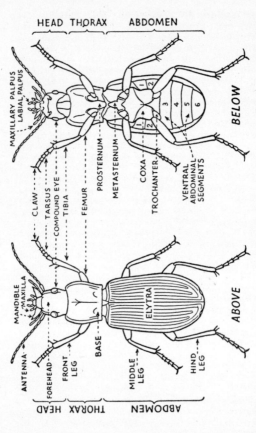

EXTERNAL STRUCTURE OF AN INSECT. The species illustrated is a widely distributed black beetle, *Feronia melanaria* (the *Pterostichus vulgaris* of older entomological literature).

legs, and usually one or two pairs of wings. Insects breathe through openings in the body (the *spiracles* or *stigmata*) connected with an intricate system of air-tubes (the *tracheae*—see Plate **4**). Most insects undergo *metamorphosis* (transformation) from *ovum* (plural, *ova*: eggs), through *larva* (plural, *larvae*: maggots, gentles, grubs, caterpillars) and *pupa* (plural, *pupae*: chrysalides) to *imago* (plural, *imagines*: adults).

THE EYES OF INSECTS

Insects have two kinds of eyes: *compound eyes* and *simple eyes* (or *ocelli*). Both types may be present in an insect, or only one kind, and many larvae have none.

The Simple Eye, or *ocellus*, is especially found in larvae, and not necessarily later in the adult insect (imago), but if present it is situated on the head between the *Compound Eyes*.

The Compound Eyes, restricted to one pair of eyes, are never found in larvae. They possess numerous facets. The House Fly has about 4,000 facets, some dragonflies have as many as 28,000. Each facet helps to form a lens, which produces an image, and although no perfect picture of surroundings can be obtained, as can be obtained with our eyes, the Compound Eye is nevertheless eminently efficient for perceiving movement of near objects. The eye is also sensitive to certain colours.

The Simple Eye is much less efficient. It gives only a rough image of near objects, its main function being to distinguish between light and darkness.

GLANDS

These organs, as in other creatures, are of extreme importance to insects. Glands produce secretions made from constituents drawn from the blood. In addition to the salivary and other glands, the following few may be noted, especially as they discharge their secretions out of the body, thus revealing their presence.

Wax Glands. A familiar example of the employment of wax is the use made of it by Bees for making honeycomb. Wax glands are also present in Bugs of the sub-order Homoptera. The secretion which is discharged as "honey-dew" by many Aphids is the best known example after that of honeycomb.

Exuvial Glands are present in the larvae of some Moths, Sawflies and Beetles, the secretion being used to help moulting. A further exudation with an analogous function is used by the Puss Moth for softening a part of its very hard pupal case just before emergence.

Silk Glands are usually situated in the head, and are used by the larvae of many insects for forming cocoons. They occur in many species of the order Lepidoptera, including the important Silkworms (species of Moths) of commerce. Caterpillars are noteworthy in having silk glands which are modified salivary glands, saliva being provided by other glands. Many members of the order Hymenoptera use silk for cocoons, and Caddisflies use it for constructing their cases.

Poison Glands. The secretions of these vary in their constituents. Poison is used for defence, paralysing or killing. In insects of the order Hymenoptera there is an acid gland and an alkaline gland, the secretions of which are combined at the time of stinging. The *setae* or "hairs" of some caterpillars are brittle, and when broken discharge an urticating liquid which can be very irritating to the skin.

Scent Glands. Secretions from these are discharged to attract the opposite sex, or their function may be to make the insect's presence acceptable to a totally different species. The larvae of many Lycaenidae (the Butterfly family of Blues, Coppers and Hairstreaks) have an odour attractive to Ants, who may be seen stroking a caterpillar's back, where the gland is situated, in order to obtain the secretion. Under this heading also may be mentioned the curious habit of *reflex-bleeding*. Some insects are able to eject blood from certain articulations ; they do this when feigning death. Such blood contains repellants of the caustic kind which make the insects distasteful as food. Certain species among the orders Hemiptera and Orthoptera are able to do this, and the same habit is especially prevalent among several beetles such as members of the genera *Meloë, Cantharis, Coccinella* and *Timarcha.*

THE PRODUCTION OF SOUND

The primary reason for the production of sound is either to attract attention or to serve as a warning to other individuals. The same reasons obtain among insects, though sound-production is often restricted to the males. Insects have no true voice, sound being made in various other ways : by *tapping* an object, by *vibrations* of various kinds, and by *friction* between different parts of the body.

The Death Watch Beetle taps its head against the floor. It does this especially from April to May, and the knocking is a sexual call. The buzzing of Bees and Beetles is in part due to the rapid vibrations of the wings. In Flies sound-production is rather more complicated, and is the subject of several theories ; certainly the rapid vibrations of the thorax, which is coupled with the wing-muscles, causes the rapid passage of air through the spiracles and is accordingly one important method of sound-production.

Besides the Cicadas, which have the most highly developed sound-producing apparatus of all insects—though we have only one very restricted species in the British Isles—the most interesting insects are our various Grasshoppers. They produce sound by friction, known as *stridulation*, and this is the commonest method. It is met with especially in the orders of the Grasshoppers, the True Bugs and the Beetles. It also happens in some Ants and even in a few Moths.

Among our Grasshoppers stridulation is restricted to the males of the families Acrididae, Tettigoniidae and Gryllidae. The Acrididae (Short-horned Grasshoppers) have a series of points on the hind legs, about eighty or ninety of them, which are rubbed against the hardened veins of the closed *tegmina* (wingcase-like fore wings). The action makes the tegmina vibrate to give a low buzzing sound. In the two other families, the Long-horned Grasshoppers and the Crickets (Gryllidae), stridulation is effected by rubbing together two specially modified parts of the hardened fore wings.

Many beetles stridulate and for this purpose parts of the body are provided with a file-and-rasp mechanism.

COLORATION OF INSECTS

We are all attracted to colours, especially when several are to be seen in one object, where they may be blended harmoniously or stand out vividly in contrast to each other. The first sympathetic study of insects must have originated from interest awakened by species exhibiting attractive colour-patterns, particularly those seen in Butterflies and Beetles, many of which were depicted in the works of early artists. The zoologist of today does not, when considering the lower animals, refer to the colours they exhibit in terms of feelings evoked, and certainly not with regard to an insect's likes or dislikes regarding them, for we have seen the danger of explanations based on making comparisons with human re-actions.

The Significance of Coloration. There has been much scientific discussion on the significance of insect coloration, and here we may state briefly that colours are not to be considered as necessarily due to some capricious act of nature. The coloration has many attributes, though it may mostly be divided roughly into warning coloration and concealing coloration. A warning coloration advertises the inedibility of an insect, such colours being black, white, yellow and red, and these colours may also be associated with aggressive insects, such as Wasps. Many other insects derive protection from predators by exhibiting colour-patterns mimicking those of inedible or aggressive species. For example, *Clytus arietis*, the Wasp Beetle (Plate **40**, *1*) displays the colours of a redoubtable stinger; the Beetle is quite harmless. Protective coloration, on the other hand, conceals the insect from detection. Examples here are the Old Lady Moth (Plate **27**) and the Lappet Moth (Plate **29**).

The Nature of Insect Coloration. White light consists of many colours, and when these are separated from each other, they display the many hues seen in a rainbow. If any colours, say the reds, are removed from white light, we shall then see only those that remain, which in this instance will be greens. Green is said to be " complementary " to red. The presence of colour therefore signifies that white light has been interfered with and this may be on account of (i) *absorption* of part of the rays, the complementary rays being reflected, and only they being visible. The absorption is determined by the pigments present in the substance illuminated. Such colours are referred to as being " pigmentary " or " chemical " ; (ii) *physical interference*, due to the structural nature of the surface illuminated. It gives rise to iridescent or " metallic " colours, known to entomologists as " structural colours ".

The two colour factors mentioned are frequently combined and are therefore referred to as " combination colours ". Structural colours are seldom found alone, and when they are combined with the pigmentary kind they produce exceedingly beautiful effects.

The necessity for field study, as in every branch of natural history, applies just as much to that of the insect colours themselves. It is a mistake to imagine that the beautiful colours of a specimen as seen in a collector's cabinet necessarily possess the same richness and variety of hues to be seen in the living insect. For example, the attractive olive-green triangular markings of the Angle Shades Moth (Plate **26**) fade after death.

CLASSIFICATION AND NOMENCLATURE

The beginner in natural history study soon realizes how essential it is to understand classification and nomenclature, not only because their existence in the world of science fulfils an obvious need, but also because of the greater enjoyment he will then derive from his observations, giving him a clearer picture of the inter-relationship of all living things.

The popular vernacular names of a particular species of insect, or indeed of any animal or plant, may differ entirely as one passes from district to district, and certainly from country to country. An occasional insect visitor from America to the south of England is the large and beautiful Milkweed Butterfly, which is also known as the Monarch. Some species may have as many as a dozen popular names, and the same names may concern two entirely different species. More often than not there is no popular name, especially for the majority of insects. The two-name (binomial) system of nomenclature, founded by Carl Linnaeus (1707–1778), ensures the accurate naming of species; it is international, and its aim is to do away with all confusion. Thus the Milkweed Butterfly is called *Danaus plexippus* Linnaeus. This last name is that of the author who first gave a scientific description of the species, in the present case, Linnaeus himself, and it may be added in full or in an abbreviated form. It was mentioned that only about a fifth of the insect population of the world has been scientifically described. As we acquire a more complete picture of the Insecta, or other forms of animal and plant life, it may happen that a revision of some nomenclature and classification becomes necessary, often to the annoyance of naturalists, and especially of beginners, who may be unaware of the many implications connected with the need for such accuracy and the respect for the historical precedence of names.*

Scientific accuracy, therefore, renders it indispensable that a system of universal naming, as distinct from the common or popular names, shall be employed. The nomenclature of species is often in Latin, two names being allocated to each species. The first signifies the **genus** (plural, genera; this is known as the generic name), and the second the **species** (this is known as the specific name). For example, the commonest of

* Scientific nomenclature is always liable to revision as knowledge of species increases. In the present book it has been deemed advisable to keep to the classification used in *A General Textbook of Entomology*, by A. D. Imms. This advanced work is the most widely consulted and may be readily found in all natural history libraries. It constitutes a veritable foundation from which specialization may begin.

all insects, the House Fly, is known as *Musca domestica* (genus *Musca*, species *domestica*). It is only in respect of a species as a whole that two names are used. A three-name (trinomial) expression is used for varieties and races of species. The Human Louse exhibits slight physical modifications according to whether it lives on the body or in the hair of the head. They are not two distinct species, but two races of the same Louse and known as *Pediculus humanus corporis* and *P. humanus capitis* respectively. A second use of three names is in respect of insects in which there are alternating generations (as among gall-causing insects), the third name then describing the form or generation.

Binomial and trinomial expressions only being given to species, all other groupings for families, super-families, sub-orders, orders and so on, are named by one word only.

The name of a **family** is obtained by adding *idae* to the root of the genus serving as the type. So we have the family Muscidae. In the same manner the **sub-family** is formed by adding *inae* to the radical: Muscinae. Our House Fly *domestica* belongs to the genus *Musca*, which is included in the sub-family Muscinae, which forms part of the family Muscidae. This family forms part of the **sub-order** Brachycera, this being one of the large divisions of the **order** Diptera, or Two-winged Flies.

The orders, such as Diptera, Hymenoptera (Ants, Bees, Wasps, etc.), Coleoptera (Beetles, etc.), are the first groupings into which the insect **class** is divided. The class Insecta, with its related classes of Arachnida, Crustacea, etc., comprise the **phylum** Arthropoda. The several phyla constitute the **Animal Kingdom.**

The Arthropoda is the most extensive of the great divisions or phyla into which the Animal

Kingdom is divided, and comprises a large assembly of animals to which the insect class belongs, as well as Crustaceans, Millipedes, Spiders and their allies, Centipedes and so on. Arthropods have an external shell-like skeleton consisting of a variable number of segments to which are attached paired jointed appendages. The skin is covered with a non-living cuticle of chitin which has to be periodically moulted as the animal grows. We are here concerned mainly with two classes, the Insecta and the Arachnida, but of the latter we have space to deal only with the interesting order of Spiders (pages 109–114).

It may here be pointed out, however, that no student of animal interdependence (which is so marked in the life-histories of Insects and Spiders) can remain for long unaware of several members of other classes included in the phylum Arthropoda. A few of the species of this exceedingly large assembly of animals are common in all gardens, rivalling Insects and Spiders as being among the best-known dwellers in our surroundings. Among those frequently to be found are Woodlice, one species of which is very well known—at least, by sight—and Millipedes and Centipedes.

These three types of Arthropoda belong to three distinct classes, the Crustacea, the Diplopoda and the Chilopoda. The following few particulars give a brief summary only of the ways in which the classes differ from each other.

The Crustacea, the class to which the terrestrial Woodlice belong, comprises mainly aquatic animals, very varied in structure, such as Lobsters, Crabs, Crayfish, Shrimps, etc. They have two pairs of antennae and at least five pairs of legs.

The Diplopoda, or Millipedes, have two pairs of legs to each segment of the body, with the exception of the first three segments. Millipedes and Centipedes appear from a cursory examination of their anatomy to be quite closely related, but in fact they are only very distant cousins.

The Chilopoda, or Centipedes, have only one pair of legs to a segment. The first pair of legs is modified into poison claws. Although " Centipede " means " hundred-footed ", the number of legs varies from fifteen to one hundred and seventy-three pairs, according to the species. The classes Diplopoda and Chilopoda have several other important differences which we need not investigate here ; however, their seemingly close relationship is the reason why they are often referred to as Myriapoda, though this is merely a term of convenience.

Arthropod classification is based mostly on observation of morphological (structural) peculiarities of external anatomy, from considerations of which naturalists are able to form groupings of closely related species.

The class INSECTA is divided into two distinct sub-classes, the *APTERYGOTA*, small wingless insects having little or no metamorphosis, and the *PTERYGOTA*, having wings and metamorphosis very varied.

The sub-class of winged insects is divided into two divisions, according to whether the wings develop internally or externally. The divisions are respectively known as the *EXOPTERYGOTA* and the *ENDOPTERYGOTA*. The tabulation on page 23 shows how the various British insects are grouped. This arrangement of the orders follows the most popular system current in the British Isles, and the reader is reminded of the footnote on page 19. However, for the advanced entomologist there is also Crowson's classification which the revisers of Imms's work have incorporated in the ninth edition of his textbook.

Orders of the Class INSECTA

Sub-Class *APTERYGOTA* (*Wingless Forms*).

Sub-Class *PTERYGOTA* (*Winged Forms*).

(a) *The division of* EXOPTERYGOTA (*Wings develop externally*).

(b) *The division of* ENDOPTERYGOTA (*Wings develop internally*).

THE SUB-CLASS *APTERYGOTA*

The three orders of primitive wingless insects included in this sub-class are of world-wide distribution. There are some 2,300 described species, and some of these are represented in the British Isles, though they are on the whole little known because of their small size and retiring habits. (They are described here on pages 24–27.) Many more species will undoubtedly be added to the list of those already known to science. These very small insects are primitive survivals and so have little metamorphosis, indeed it is often absent; any change that does occur is gradual.

Order THYSANURA. *Bristle-tails*

Description. All small insects. Mouth-parts adapted for biting. Antennae long, many-jointed. Compound eyes present or absent. Abdomen 11-segmented. Metamorphosis wanting or gradual. Colour brown, grey or white.

Classification. Two sub-orders: *ECTO-GNATHA*, having exserted mouth-parts, and *ENTOGNATHA*, having mouth-parts sunk within the head. (The Bristle-tails may be divided into two distinct orders, the *DIPLURA*, having two long *cerci* or "tails", and the *THYSANURA*, having three long cerci.) (23 British species.)

In this widely distributed order are included the most primitive insects alive today. They are little known to amateur naturalists, and relatively few experts have studied them. Bristle-tails live under stones, in rotting wood, under wallpaper

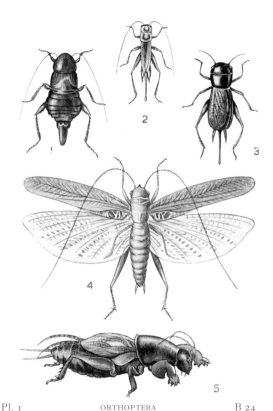

1. Cockroach, *Blatta orientalis*, female. 2. House Cricket, *Gryllulus domesticus*. 3. Field Cricket, *Gryllus campestris*. 4. Great Green Grasshopper, *Tettigonia viridissima*. 5. Mole Cricket, *Gryllotalpa gryllotalpa*. (*All natural size, except 4—slightly reduced.*) Pages 28 *to* 31.

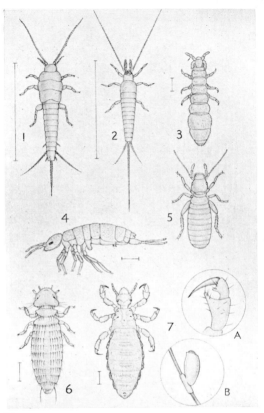

Pl. 2   WINGLESS INSECTS

1. Silver-fish, *Lepisma saccharina*, p. 25.   2. *Petrobius maritimus*, p. 25.   3. *Anurida maritima*, p. 27.   4. Spring-tail, p. 27.   5. *Liposcelis granicola*, p. 35.   6. Chicken Louse, *Menopon pallidum*, p. 36.   7. Human Louse, *Pediculus humanus:*   *A*—foreleg claw, *B*—egg or nit glued to hair (*both considerably enlarged*); *pages* 36–37.

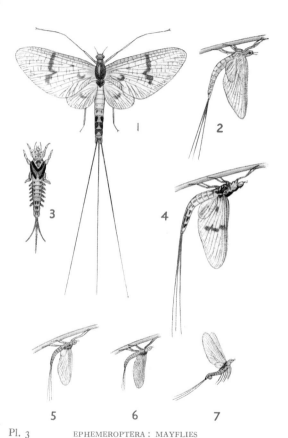

Pl. 3   EPHEMEROPTERA : MAYFLIES

Family Ephemeridae : *Ephemera danica*—1. Female
imago " set " ; 2. Male sub-imago ; 3. Nymph.
4. *E. vulgata*, female imago.   Family Ephemerellidae :
Ephemerella ignita—5. Male imago (the fisherman's
" Sherry Spinner ") ; 6. Male sub-imago (" Blue-
winged Dun ") ; 7. Female imago (" Sherry Spinner ").
(*All natural size.*)   *Pages* 37–38.

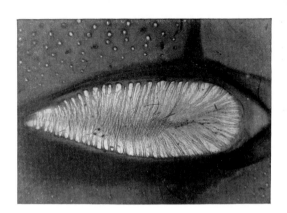

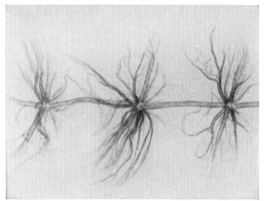

Pl. 4   THE BREATHING OF INSECTS

Insects breathe through openings in the body, the spiracles or stigmata (*above*), connected with an intricate system of air-tubes, the tracheae (*below : both greatly enlarged*); *p.* 13.

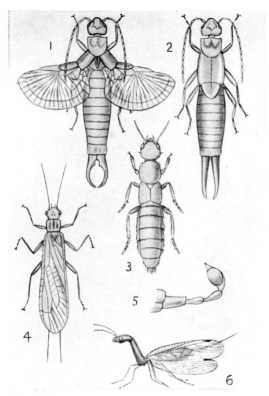

Pl. 5   DERMAPTERA, COLEOPTERA, PLECOPTERA,
MECOPTERA, NEUROPTERA-MEGALOPTERA

DERMAPTERA : Common Earwig, *Forficula auricularia*
(*approx.* × 4): 1. Male, wings extended; 2. Female,
wings folded beneath wing-cases; *p.* 32.   3. Beetles
of the family Staphylinidae (*p.* 84) also have reduced wing-cases, but no pincers. (*Sizes vary.*)
PLECOPTERA : 4. Stonefly, *Perla maxima* (*natural size*),
p. 34.   MECOPTERA : 5. Scorpion-fly, extremity of male
abdomen (*greatly enlarged*), *p.* 58.   NEUROPTERA-
MEGALOPTERA: 6. Snakefly, *Raphidia notata* (×2), *p.* 56.

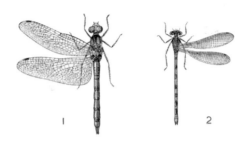

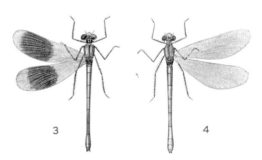

Pl. 6   ODONATA :
DRAGONFLIES, DEMOISELLE-FLIES

1. *Sympetrum striolatum*, male (39 *to* 43 *mm.*, $1\frac{9}{16}$ *to* $1\frac{11}{16}$ *in.*). 2. *Enallagma cyathigerum*, male (31 *to* 33 mm., $1\frac{1}{4}$ *to* $1\frac{5}{16}$ *in.*). *Agrion splendens*—3. Male (44 *to* 48 *mm.*, $1\frac{3}{4}$ *to* $1\frac{7}{8}$ *in.*); 4. Female (43 *to* 46 *mm.*, $1\frac{11}{16}$ *to* $1\frac{13}{16}$ *in.*). *Pages* 42, 43, 45.

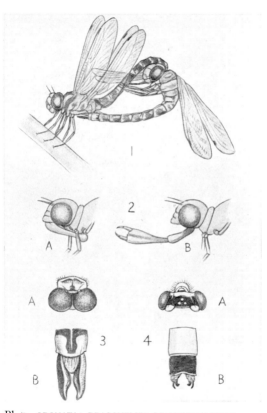

Pl. 7 ODONATA: DRAGONFLIES, DEMOISELLE-FLIES

1. Pairing of Dragonflies. 2. "Mask" of Dragonfly nymph at rest (*A*) and extended (*B*). 3. Head of Dragonfly, *Anax imperator*—A ($\times$ 1$\frac{1}{2}$), anal clasper—B ($\times$ 2$\frac{1}{2}$). 4. Head of Demoiselle-fly, *Enallagma cyathigerum*—A ($\times$ 3$\frac{1}{2}$), anal clasper—B ($\times$ 10). *Pages* 40–41.

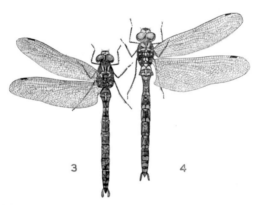

Pl. 8   ODONATA: B 25
DRAGONFLIES, DEMOISELLE-FLIES

1. *Agrion virgo*, male (45 to 47 *mm.*, $1\frac{3}{4}$ to $1\frac{7}{8}$ *in.*).
2. *Pyrrhosoma nymphula*, female (35 to 37 *mm.*, $1\frac{3}{8}$ to
$1\frac{1}{2}$ *in.*).   3. *Aeshna juncea*, male (73 to 76 *mm.*, $2\frac{7}{8}$ to
3 *in.*).   4. *A. cyanea*, male (74 *mm.*, $2\frac{15}{16}$ *in.*). *Pages*
42, 43, 44.

and amongst the dead leaves in woods, as well as in the soil. They are also to be found in the nests of Ants, as well as (abroad) in those of Termites. The best known is *Lepisma saccharina*, the common Silver-fish (Plate **2**, *1*), which finds its way into our houses from grocery stores, or in paper and books, to which it is destructive. There is also an interesting species, *Petrobius maritimus* (Plate **2**, *2*), which is found among rocks near the edge of the sea along the British coast. The baker's " Fire Brat ", *Thermobia domestica*, also belongs to this order ; it is remarkable for the heat it can bear. The food of Bristle-tails consists especially of sugars, starches, leaf mould and humus.

The three species mentioned belong to the sub-order *Ectognatha*.

The second sub-order, *Entognatha*, comprises one genus, *Campodea*, among which is included the minute species *Campodea silvestrii* (the *C. staphylinus* of older entomological literature). The structure of the larvae of many insects resembles in form that of this very primitive insect, and this has given rise to the term *campodeiform*. Such larvae have the head, thorax and abdomen well-defined, and they possess only three pairs of legs ; they are active in habit. An example is the larva of the Great Diving Beetle, *Dytiscus marginalis* (Plate **33**, *4*). The other type of larva is termed *eruciform;* in this the three major divisions are not evident, and in addition to the thoracic legs there may be prolegs. Examples of this eruciform type are shown in the larvae of Lepidoptera (Butterflies and Moths) illustrated on Plate **24**. Many eruciform larvae, however, have no legs, or, where legs are present, they may be only vestigial ; examples of this type are the larvae of Diptera (True Flies) illustrated on Plate **54**.

Order PROTURA (MYRIENTOMATA). No popular name

Description. Very small species. Mouthparts sunk within the head and adapted for piercing. Antennae and compound eyes wanting. Abdomen 12-segmented. Metamorphosis slight.

Classification. The species of this order are divided into two families. (17 British species.)

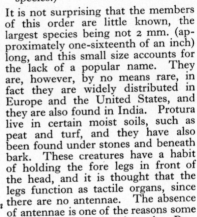

Acerentomon doderoi

It is not surprising that the members of this order are little known, the largest species being not 2 mm. (approximately one-sixteenth of an inch) long, and this small size accounts for the lack of a popular name. They are, however, by no means rare, in fact they are widely distributed in Europe and the United States, and they are also found in India. Protura live in certain moist soils, such as peat and turf, and they have also been found under stones and beneath bark. These creatures have a habit of holding the fore legs in front of the head, and it is thought that the legs function as tactile organs, since there are no antennae. The absence of antennae is one of the reasons some naturalists maintain that the Protura form a class of their own, the Myrientomata. The figure illustrating Protura is *Acerentomon doderoi* (much magnified).

Order COLLEMBOLA. *Spring-tails*

Description. Mouth-parts sunk within the head, principally adapted for biting. Antennae usually 4-jointed. Abdomen 6-segmented mostly with 3 pairs of appendages. No metamorphosis. Colour varies from white to black; there are also green, yellow, red and some banded species.

Classification. Two sub-orders, ARTHRO-PLEONA, having segmentation of the abdomen well defined, and SYMPHLEONA, having vestigial or no segmentation of abdomen. (261 British species.)

Spring-tails are named after their method of leaping to a distance of several inches when disturbed. They congregate in vast numbers. A well-known entomologist, John Ford, found that an acre of meadow-land, to a depth of 9 inches, contained 230,000,000 of these insects. They are also to be found beneath the bark of trees, in decaying vegetable matter, and so on, especially if conditions are moist. Spring-tails render invaluable help in sewage farms, where they feed on decaying matter. *Anurida maritima* (Plate **2**, *3*), lives along the coast and is submerged at high tide. It is one of the few marine insects; it has not the modified springing legs characteristic of other Collembola (Plate **2**, *4*).

The Spring-tail *Hydropura aquatica*, described by Linnaeus as long ago as 1758, was one of the favourite "objects of the microscope" prepared for sale during the heyday of amateur microscopy in the last century. Members of the species are found on stagnant pools, where they may be seen jerking about on the surface of the water.

Most species are small, rarely exceeding a length of 5 mm. (three-sixteenths of an inch).

THE SUB-CLASS *PTERYGOTA*

The remaining insect orders described in this book all form part of the second sub-class, the *PTERYGOTA*, or Winged Insects. The absence of wings in several species is due to their loss through highly evolved specialization, often bringing about actual degeneration.

The *PTERYGOTA* develop their wings either externally (*EXOPTERYGOTA*: pages 28–54), or internally (*ENDOPTERYGOTA*: pages 55–106). In the latter the wings become visible only in the adult (imago) stage.

Division (a), *EXOPTERYGOTA*

Order ORTHOPTERA. *Grasshoppers, Crickets, Cockroaches*

Description. Mouth-parts adapted for biting or chewing. Usually four wings, the fore pair being modified into hardened wing-cases which protect the hind pair when at rest. Hind wings membranous and transparent. Abdomen with jointed cerci or " tails ", but not always evident. Ovipositor generally present. Metamorphosis slight or absent. Colour, browns, greens.

Classification. This order is readily divided into *CURSORIA*, Runners, and *SALTATORIA*, Jumpers. (38 British species.)

The *CURSORIA*, the *Runners*, are represented in the British Isles by the unpleasant Cockroaches (family Blattidae). Most of these insects are actually natives of frost-free habitats which have become established here, but only where continuous warmth is assured, such as in bakeries, hotel kitchens and at zoological gardens in animal cages which are kept at warm temperatures. They are most readily seen behind the glass where snakes are kept, and seem actually to be " tame " there and, contrary to their usual habits, forget that they are supposed to be nocturnal. Here they may certainly be studied at leisure. The female lays her eggs in an egg-case (*ootheca*) which may sometimes be seen projecting from the abdomen. An example of such a female is shown in the illustration of our commonest species, *Blatta orientalis* (Plate **I**, *1*). Observing the long and many-jointed antennae of a living Cockroach, and the way they are moved about nervously and deliberately, we can deduce the very great importance of these organs to the insect.

Cockroaches eat all kinds of foods, especially those that are sweet and starchy. They are destructive pests, and they foul stored foodstuffs, being particularly obnoxious because of their stink-glands. The unpleasant smell of Cockroaches persists wherever they have been.

The *SALTATORIA*, or *Jumpers*, are represented by true native species, for they include our common summer-loving Grasshoppers and tiresome House Crickets. They differ essentially from Cockroaches in having the third pair of legs powerfully developed for jumping and leaping, these limbs being most important for allowing the nymphs, which cannot yet fly, to escape from danger by leaping. Furthermore, many species remain wingless on reaching the adult stage. Grasshoppers emerge in May from eggs laid the previous year in capsules of dried mucus ; they are fully grown by midsummer and live until September.

There are two kinds of Grasshopper in the British Isles, the Short-horned and the Long-horned, named after the length of the antennae. The Short-horned, of which we have fourteen native species, belong to the family Acrididae.

They are vegetarians, and include some of our commonest species. They are also the noisiest of our Grasshoppers. The volume of their " song " or stridulation (pages 15–16) is in direct proportion to the heat and amount of sunshine, and they are indeed our summer songsters, the equivalent of the Mediterranean Cicadas. These Acridids occur in all parts of the world and some of them are among the greatest of all insect pests, for the foreign locusts are of their number. One of our commonest species is *Omocestus viridulus* which will be found especially on the grassy slopes of downs. It is dull olive-green in colour.

Our Long-horned species belong to the family Tettigoniidae, and are also popularly known as Bush Crickets. They differ in several respects from the Short-horned. Besides the obvious difference in length of antennae, they have their ears situated in the fore legs. The Short-horned have their ears or (membranous) tympana situated on the first abdominal segment. The method of stridulation is also quite different. The Long-horned rub parts of the wings together, as we have already seen, whereas the Short-horned use their legs on the fore-wings for the purpose. The Long-horned are not specialized in diet and are very frequently carnivorous, attacking other insects as well as their own kind. They do their hunting mainly at night and bite the victim just behind the neck. The largest of our Grasshoppers belongs to this family; it is *Tettigonia viridissima*, the Great Green Grasshopper (Plate 1, 4), in which the method of pairing is among the most curious of the insect world and has been described at length by the incomparable Fabre.

The Crickets (family Gryllidae), although closely related to the Long-horned Grasshoppers, may be distinguished from them and the other foregoing species by their long cerci (" tails "), and by the hardened fore wings, which lie flat over the abdomen, and downwards along the sides. Furthermore, the right fore wing lies over the left, which is contrary to what usually obtains in this order. The stridulating apparatus is also relatively larger than in the Long-horned Grass-hoppers. The best known of the Crickets is *Gryllulus domesticus* (Plate **1**, *2*), the House Cricket, also known as the Cricket on the Hearth. It is found fairly frequently in or near warm places. There is also the lesser known *Gryllus campestris* (Plate **1**, *3*), a field species which has a burrow home, and which is the insect made famous by Fabre's description of its habits. This species, popularly known as the Field Cricket, is black in colour with a yellow band across the base of the elytra; the head is big and broad. It will be found sitting at the mouth of its lair chirping away merrily on hot days from the middle of May to the middle of July.

The most unusual Cricket in appearance is *Gryllotalpa gryllotalpa* (Plate **1**, *5*), the Mole Cricket (family Gryllotalpidae). It is infrequently seen because of its subterranean habits, but is a most interesting species, showing much morphological modification. The strong fore legs have become adapted for burrowing and, with the front part of the body, which is armoured, are therefore in keeping with its habits. The Mole Cricket lays her eggs in a mass, placing them in a cavity and remaining in attendance. However, when the eggs hatch, the parent seems to destroy some of the progeny. Gilbert White, in his *Natural History of Selborne*, gives a most interesting account of finding the " nest " or egg-mass of this insect.

Order DERMAPTERA. *Earwigs*

Description. Long body. Biting mouth-parts. Antennae long, many-jointed. Fore wings modified into short wing-cases, hind wings folded and for flying. Many wingless forms. Cerci unjointed, forming the familiar pincers or forceps. Metamorphosis slight or absent. Colour, browns and black.

Classification. Three sub-orders, only one, the FORFICULINA, Earwigs, being represented in the British Isles. The others, the ARIXENINA and HEMIMERINA, are tropical and all species are blind external parasites of bats and rats. (9 British species of earwigs.)

Our commonest Earwig, *Forficula auricularia* (Plate **5**, *1*, shown with wings extended) is so decidedly distinctive in appearance that we recognize it at the first glance. It is not often that a creature of mostly nocturnal habit is so well known, even to non-naturalists. In daylight it conceals itself, often among the petals of flowers, particularly when these are large and luxuriant, as in the case of dahlias, and thus it is that Earwigs are frequently disturbed and seen. The name " Earwig " too helps us to bear it well in mind, although to the scientist it is puzzling. It is thought to have its origin in the fact that these insects could wander into the ear of a person at rest, the ear cavity being a suitable place for concealment. Should this occur, it certainly results in consternation and physical irritation, but that they are actually Ear-piercers, as they are called in French, is considered to be mere calumniation of a highly interesting insect.

Earwigs have no constriction between the thorax and the abdomen, but the most marked features are the forceps or pincers which terminate the abdomen (Plate 5, *1, 2*). There is much variation in the shape of the pincers, and they also differ between the sexes, those of the female being less curved. There are several theories regarding the use of these instruments. They are often thought to be organs of offence and defence, for they may sometimes be seen projecting jaw-like in places where the insect is hiding, and an Earwig may certainly be seen raising the pincers when alarmed. It has also been said that the pincers are used for folding and unfolding the wings. The wings are complicated, and seem to be infrequently used, and are remarkable for the manner in which they are literally folded and tucked away under the wing-cases.

The Common Earwig is found throughout the British Isles and remarkable observations have been made about it. Hibernation occurs in the adult stage and usually a male and a female are found together. They will be found in small galleries, under stones and other sheltered places. Here pairing occurs frequently. Eggs are laid between January and March ; the male then leaves the nest, perhaps driven away. The Earwig lays comparatively few eggs, about two dozen. They are smooth and pale coloured, and they are brooded over by the female very much as in the case of the hen. The eggs are laid in mid-winter, under a stone or other suitable cover, but always in a damp situation. Here the eggs would soon be attacked by mildew were this not prevented by the mother, who licks each egg clean once every day.

The life-history of the Earwig was studied as long ago as the middle of the eighteenth century by Baron de Geer. He scattered the eggs, and found that the female collected them together again, carrying them in her mouth. On hatching, the young remain with their mother and place themselves " under her belly, like little chicks under a hen ", which was what had originally

C
33

attracted this naturalist to study Earwigs more closely.

Order PLECOPTERA. *Stoneflies*

Description. Moderate sized or large insects. Body soft. Long antennae. Weak biting mouth-parts. Four membranous wings with numerous veins; wings held flat over body when at rest. Abdomen usually with long jointed cerci ("tails"). Metamorphosis incomplete, pupal stage absent. Nymphs aquatic. Colour brown.

Classification. A small order, three of the seven families, as classified by Imms, being represented in the British Isles. (32 British species.)

Stoneflies are on the whole little known to the majority of people. This is due to the rather restricted habitat of these insects. Their aquatic larvae require clean, well-oxygenated water. They are found beneath the stones of mountain streams, and near waterfalls. The nymphs climb out of the water when full-grown, and the final transformation into the imago then takes place, very much in the manner of Dragonflies.

The adults are fairly large. What makes them also particularly noticeable to the non-naturalist is that their flight attracts attention to itself by its slowness ; the insects are weak fliers, and when touched they fall to the ground. Stoneflies never wander far from water, and will be found at rest on anything suitable in the neighbourhood, including stones, fences, bridges and so on. The adults are short-lived, like Mayflies, and apparently they do not feed, the mouth-parts being almost useless. The female usually lays her eggs in one mass, and in some species there may be as many as 2,000 eggs. These become detached from each other in the water, and eventually adhere to stones and plants by means of a long thread with which each egg is provided.

Stoneflies may be readily distinguished from members of the order Neuroptera (page 55) by the cerci (" tails ") present in the adults. Also the wings are held flat over the body (Plate **5**, *4*), whilst Neuroptera hold them roof-wise.

Order PSOCOPTERA. *Booklice*

Description. Very small insects. Biting mouth-parts. Winged or wingless. Long antennae, having nine or more joints. Membranous wings. Segments of thorax very distinct. Metamorphosis gradual or absent.

Classification. Two sub-orders, the ZORAPTERA and the *PSOCIDA*, to which the British species belong; the latter is sometimes regarded as a distinct order. (68 British species.)

The first of the sub-orders is of no importance to us in Britain; to it belong the tiny insects that have the nine-segmented antennae and very short cerci (" tails "). Cerci are absent in Psocida, and the antennae have many segments, from twenty to as many as fifty. At times species of Psocida may be very numerous indeed, especially in undisturbed places, such as in empty houses. Many are gregarious in habit.

Among the sub-order Psocida are the very minute whitish creatures (*Liposcelis divinatorius*) found in old books and papers. They are the Booklice, whose food consists of book-paste as well as decaying vegetable and animal matter. Not all of our native species have the same feeding habits ; some live on dry farm refuse and a number of stored cereals, others live out of doors on tree-trunks, fences, beneath bark, on moss, lichen and other vegetation. Psocids are important distributors of spores of fungi. Some forms are winged, and are easily confused with aphids. A wingless example of the order is *Liposcelis granicola* (Plate **2**, *5*).

35

Order ANOPLURA. *Lice*

Description. Small flattened insects. Wingless. Antennae short, 3- to 5-jointed. Mouthparts adapted for biting, or for piercing and sucking. Thoracic segments indistinct. Legs short and adapted for clinging to host. No metamorphosis. Parasites of mammals and birds. Colour whitish-yellow or darker.

Classification. Two sub-orders, *MALLOPHAGA*, Biting Lice, and *SIPHUNCULATA*, Sucking Lice. The status of these two divisions may be raised to that of separate orders, the main difference between them being concerned with the method of feeding, whether the species bites or sucks—the anatomical features of the mouth-parts constituting great differences where classification is concerned. (286 British species.)

Species of one sub-order, Mallophaga, the Biting Lice, are found mostly on birds, and are well known to bird fanciers. A few species are found on mammals. Biting Lice feed on the products of the skin. In birds they are particularly destructive to the feathers, and in severe cases this may result in bald patches. The very common *Menopon pallidum* or Chicken Louse (Plate 2, 6) is a pest of chickens. Ducks are infested with *Philopterus dentatus* but there are also several other lice parasites. Cats may have among their fur *Felicola subrostratus* and dogs *Trichodectes canis*.

Members of the other sub-order, the Siphunculata, or Sucking Lice, feed on the blood of mammals, each species having its particular kind of louse. The Human Louse, *Pediculus humanus* (Plate 2, 7), has two races, according to whether it lives on the head (sub-species or race *capitis*) or on the body (race *corporis*). The species is of great medical importance as a vector (disease carrier-

36

transmitter) of more diseases than any other insect, including such scourges as typhus, trench fever and so on. One other species also lives on man—the Crab Louse, *Phthirus pubis*, particularly restricted to unclean people. *Pediculus* infection may originate temporarily from unclean people conveying it to others in crowded conditions in which customary cleanliness cannot be practised, as among front-line troops and prisoners.

Lice cannot live away from their host, and their highly specialized habits are reflected in their structure, such as the absence of wings and the powerful clinging-claws (Plate **2**, 7*A*). Lice glue their eggs (" nits ") to the host's hairs (Plate **2**, 7*B*), or to clothing, and they hatch in about eight days.

Order EPHEMEROPTERA. *Mayflies*

Description. Body soft. Mouth-parts vestigial. Antennae short and bristly. Abdomen long terminating in three long cerci (" tails "). Four membranous wings, transparent, with many veins, the hind pair much reduced in size. Wings held vertically upwards when at rest. Metamorphosis incomplete but unique in that the imagines (adults) have a winged sub-imago stage. Nymphs aquatic.

Classification. The order comprises thirteen families, eight of which are British. They are grouped into three superfamilies. (45 British species.)

Mayflies (Plate **3**) are common round the margins of inland waters. They may often be seen in large swarms at the end of May and the beginning of June. They are particularly well known to anglers, who refer to them as " duns ", " spinners " and " drakes ". These are used as bait, and artificial copies of them are made to serve the same purpose. All anglers' " flies " are not May-flies, for they also include Stoneflies and Caddis-flies, though the majority of species do belong to the order Ephemeroptera.

The brief life of a Mayfly is proverbial. It may last but a few hours, though this is of course true only of the adult winged form. The nymph, which is entirely aquatic, may have lived as long as three years before completing its larval stage of development. An example is the nymph of *Ephemera danica* (Plate **3**, *3*).

The nymphs vary much in form, depending on whether they live in still or in running water, and this has a direct bearing on the genera to be found there. The nymphs feed mainly on minute vegetable matter, such as algae and diatoms, in addition to fragments of other plant tissues. Some species prefer to live where there are sandy beds, whilst others are to be found in silt or moss, in the decaying vegetation of ditches, in fact, almost everywhere. They breathe by means of tracheal gills, which vary much in form and are attached externally to the abdominal segments.

The fully developed nymph floats to the surface of the water in late spring or early summer, or it climbs out on to a stone or up a plant. Here the nymphal case splits open, and from it emerges a winged insect, but unlike the similar process in other insects, this is not yet the final stage of its life-history. It has only attained the stage known as the sub-imago, unique in insect metamorphosis. The sub-imago is dull-coloured ; it is the " dun " of the angler (Plate **3**, *6*). It flies away to rest among vegetation, and after a while the final moult takes place, disclosing the fully-coloured Mayfly or " spinner " (Plate **3**, *5, 7*).

Swarms of males of many species engage in a dancing flight, which is a rhythmic up-and-down movement, and takes place at certain times of the day. On the approach of a female some of the males go towards her; pairing takes place in " nuptial flight ". Many Mayflies are nocturnal in habit.

The eggs are dropped into the water, or the abdomen is dipped below the surface, and in some species the insect actually penetrates into the water to lay her eggs. Mayfly eggs are remarkable for the diversity of their structure.

Order ODONATA. *Dragonflies, Demoiselle-flies*

Description. Large or moderate sized predaceous insects. Body long, often slender. Head large with very large and prominent eyes. Antennae thin and very short. Four wings approximately same size and membranous with many veins. Metamorphosis incomplete. Nymphs aquatic.

Classification. Two distinct sub-orders : the ANISOPTERA, Dragonflies, hold the wings open when at rest, the fore wings differing in shape from the hind pair, which are broader near the base. The space between the eyes is always smaller than their own diameter. The ZYGO-PTERA, Demoiselle-flies, close their wings (with very few exceptions) vertically above the abdomen when at rest. Fore and hind wings resemble each other closely, their bases being narrow. Nymphs have three tail-like projections which are gills, absent in nymphs of Anisoptera. There is a third sub-order, the ANISOZYGOPTERA, having few living representative species, and none British. (42 British species.)

The brilliantly coloured, sun-loving Dragonfly is noted for the speed of its flight—in one species this is said to attain sixty miles an hour ! It is a fearsome hunter of other insects which are caught and devoured in flight. The Demoiselle-fly is a much more delicate insect, and may even be quite a weak flier. It is certainly not the countryman's "Horse Stinger" or "Devil's Darning Needle", popular names which must assuredly have been given by non-naturalists to the much more powerful species of Dragonflies (sub-order Anisoptera), though no member of the order Odonata has a sting. Of the Dragonflies, *Libellula quadrimaculata* (Plate **9**, *4*) is an example of a migratory species, large numbers of them having been recorded as travelling many miles out to sea, though on the whole Dragonflies do not wander far from their breeding-place ; many may, however, frequently be found farther from stretches of water than the majority of insects having aquatic larvae. Demoiselle-flies are normally found only near water.

The nymphs of this order are well known to collectors of pond life. Specimens are popular though often very destructive inmates of an amateur's aquarium, and their habits at this stage of their life-history are therefore better known than are those of the adult insect. Nymphs of the two sub-orders are easily distinguishable from each other, for the Dragonfly nymph has a more robust structure (Plate **10**, *7*, *8*, *9*, also Plate **12**), than that of the Demoiselle-fly (Plate **10**, *1* to *6*), which is slender, and has in addition three long "tails" which are breathing gills. Both nymphs are carnivorous, possessing a "mask" (Plate **7**, *2*), consisting of impaling mandibles or hooks on an extensible limb, which is used for bringing the food to the mouth and for holding it there. The mask is shown at rest, *A*, and extended, *B* ; it is shot out with lightning speed when prey of suitable size approaches within reach, and the nymph may also dart forward to seize its victim, but at other times the creature is sluggish. It is difficult to detect

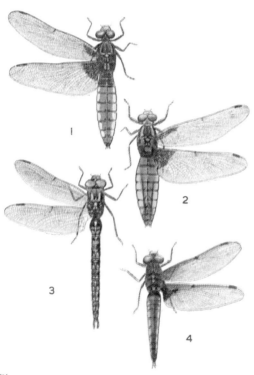

Pl. 9   ODONATA : DRAGONFLIES   C 40

Libellula depressa—1. Male (47 *mm.*, $1\frac{7}{8}$ *in.*); 2. Female (42 to 44 *mm.*, $1\frac{5}{8}$ to $1\frac{3}{4}$ *in.*).   3. *Brachytron pratense*, male (58 *mm.*, $2\frac{5}{16}$ *in.*).   4. *Libellula quadrimaculata*, male (39 to 47 *mm.*, $1\frac{9}{16}$ to $1\frac{7}{8}$ *in.*). *Pages* 40, 43, 44, 45.

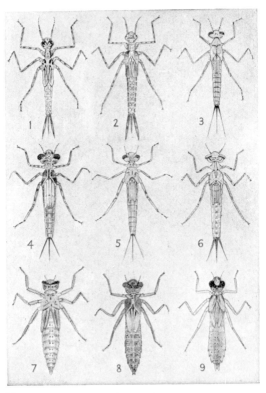

Pl. 10   ODONATA :

DEMOISELLE-FLY NYMPHS : 1. *Agrion virgo* (32 mm.,
$1\frac{1}{4}$ in.). 2. *A. splendens* (32 mm., $1\frac{1}{4}$ in.). 3. *Lestes
sponsa* (26 mm., 1 in.). 4. *Pyrrhosoma nymphula* (19 mm.,
$\frac{3}{4}$ in.). 5. *Ischnura elegans* (20 mm., $\frac{3}{4}$ in.). 6. *Enallagma cyathigerum* (20 mm., $\frac{3}{4}$ in.). DRAGONFLY NYMPHS :
7. *Cordulegaster boltonii* (41 mm., $1\frac{5}{8}$ in.). 8. *Brachytron
pratense* (40 mm., $1\frac{9}{16}$ in.). 9. *Anax imperator* (54 mm.,
$2\frac{3}{16}$ in.). *Pages* 42–43.

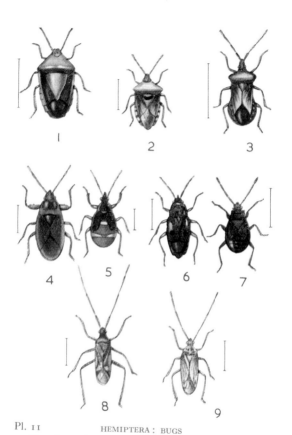

Pl. 11   HEMIPTERA : BUGS

1. *Piezodorus lituratus*. 2. *Elasmostethus interstinctus*.
3. *Coreus marginatus*. 4. *Gastrodes grossipes*; 5. Its
nymph. 6. *Pyrrhocoris apterus*; 7. Its nymph. 8.
Phytocoris ulmi. 9. *Calocoris ochromelas*. Pages 47–48.

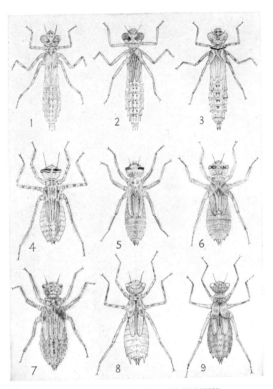

Pl. 12   ODONATA : DRAGONFLY NYMPHS

1. *Aeshna cyanea* (48 mm., 1⅞ in.).   2. *A. juncea* (43 mm., 1 11/16 in.).   3. *A. grandis* (43 mm., 1⅞ in.).   4. *Cordulia aenea* (22 mm., ⅞ in.).   5. *Orthetrum coerulescens* (19 mm., ¾ in.).   6. *Libellula quadrimaculata* (26 mm., 1 in.).   7. *L. depressa* (25 mm., 1 in.).   8. *Sympetrum striolatum* (18 mm., ¾ in.).   9. *S. scoticum* (16 mm., ⅝ in.).   *Pages* 44–45.

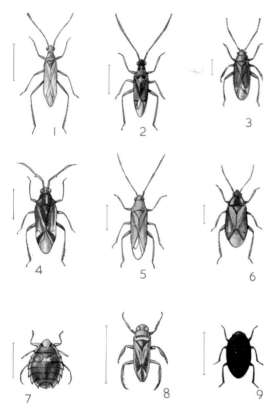

Pl. 13   HEMIPTERA-HETEROPTERA, HEMIPTERA-
HOMOPTERA: BUGS

HEMIPTERA-HETEROPTERA : 1. *Dicyphus epilobii.* 2.
Cyllecoris histrionicus. 3. *Orthotylus ericetorum.* 4.
Harpocera thoracica. Pages 48–49. 5. *Phylus pallipes.* 6. *Psallus variabilis.* Pages 48–49. WATER BUGS: 7. *Aphelocheirus aestivalis.* 8. *Notonecta glauca.* Pages 50, 51. HEM-
IPTERA-HOMOPTERA: 9. Froghopper, *Cercopis vulnerata,*
p. 52.

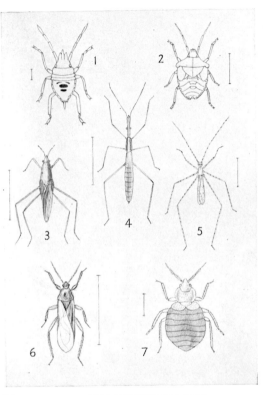

Pl. 14   HEMIPTERA-HETEROPTERA : BUGS

1 and 2. Nymphs of *Acanthosoma haemorrhoidale.*
3. *Gerris gibbifer.* 4. *Hydrometra stagnorum.* 5.
Empicoris vagabundus. 6. *Reduvius personatus.* 7. Bed
Bug, *Cimex lectularius.* Pages 48–50.

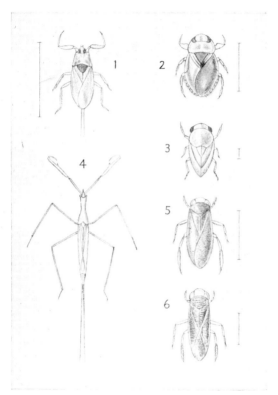

Pl. 15   HEMIPTERA-HETEROPTERA,
           (CRYPTOCERATA) : BUGS

1. *Nepa cinerea.* 2. *Ilyocoris* (= *Naucoris*) *cimicoides.*
3. *Plea leachi.* 4. *Ranatra linearis* (*natural size*).
5. *Corixa punctata.* 6. *C.* (= *Sigara*) *striata. Pages*
50–51.

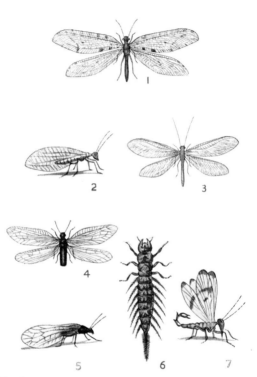

Pl. 16   NEUROPTERA, MECOPTERA

NEUROPTERA: 1. Brown Lacewing, *Osmylus fulvice-phalus*, "set". Green Lacewing, *Chrysopa carnea*—
2. At rest; 3. With wings "set". Alderfly, *Sialis lutaria*—4. "Set"; 5. At rest; 6. Larva. (*All approx. natural size.*) *Pages* 56–58. MECOPTERA: 7. Scorpion-fly, *Panorpa communis* (*natural size*), male, *p.* 59.

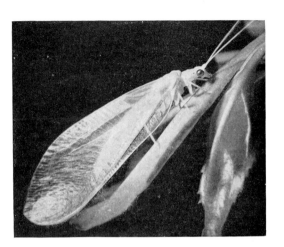

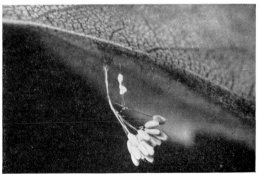

Pl. 17   THE LACEWING—A BENEFICIAL INSECT

Above : Adult; *below :* Eggs on the underside of a leaf (*both much enlarged*); *p.* 57.

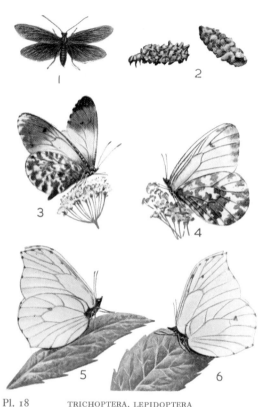

Pl. 18   TRICHOPTERA, LEPIDOPTERA

TRICHOPTERA : Caddisfly, *Phryganea grandis*—1. Imago ;
2. Larva cases ; *p.* 60.   LEPIDOPTERA : Orange-tip—
3. Male ; 4. Female.   Brimstone Butterfly—5. Male ;
6. Female.   *Pages* 64–65.

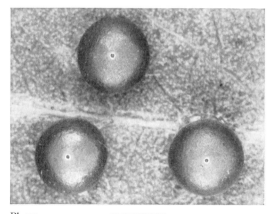

Pl. 19   LEPIDOPTERA

Above : Eggs of Vapourer Moth (× 6).   *Below :* Eggs
of Puss Moth (× 14).   *Pages* 75, 76.

Pl. 20   LEPIDOPTERA: GARDEN BUTTERFLIES   C 41

1. Peacock, male.   2. Small Tortoiseshell, male.   3
and 4. Holly Blue, male and female.   5. Comma, male.
(*All natural size.*)   *Pages* 65–66.

a nymph because it possesses most effective protective coloration, and this may even change according to environment.

Some of the more common nymphs found when collecting from ponds are shown in Plates **10** and **12**. Although metamorphosis is incomplete in this order, it will be seen from these two plates that the fully grown nymphs do not bear a close resemblance to the adult insects (Plates **6**, **8** and **9**), as is the case, for example, in Grasshoppers and Bugs. This is particularly evident in the Dragon-flies, whose robust nymphal body does not announce the slenderness of that of the adult, nor does it indicate—as in the case of most insects—any of the wonderful coloration to come.

The nymph leaves the water after a larval period of about a year in the case of the Demoiselle-flies (Zygoptera) and two years in that of the Dragon-flies (Anisoptera). It then climbs up a reed or other projection above the surface. Here the final transformation takes place, the nymphal skin splits and the imago wriggles out. The wings then expand and the abdomen becomes elongate and slender ; the coloration takes a certain time to develop, and this waiting or " teneral " period may last for several days.

The mating of the adults (Plate **7**, *1*) is most curious. It takes place in flight, on the ground, or among vegetation, depending on the genus. The male has special anal claspers (Plate **7**, *3B*, *4B*), which are used for gripping the female in the back of the head or neck. The extraordinary pairing attitude adopted in this order of Odonata is necessary because the orifices of the male and female genitalia are situated at widely separated parts of the body.

The eggs are laid in water, sometimes inside plant stems. The females of some species penetrate below the surface for egg-laying, and are helped in doing this by the male, who remains above the surface whilst keeping a firm grasp on the female.

As the nymphal instar (stage) is more often studied than the adult instar (because it is possible to confine nymphs most conveniently in an aquarium where they may be kept under close observation), we give below a few details of some of the commoner nymphs collected from ponds and streams.

Nymphs of Demoiselle-flies (sub-order ZYGOPTERA)

(The measurements given of nymphs indicate the length of the body, including the tail-like gills, but excluding the antennae. Where equivalent measurements are given in inches, these are approximate, to the nearest sixteenth of an inch.)

Agrion virgo (Plate **10**, *1*). Attains 32 mm. (1¼ in.). Widely distributed and very common in the South. Prefers swift running water, but also found in ponds. Imago on the wing in spring and summer, most common in June and July. The male (Plate **8**, *1*) is the most beautiful of the Demoiselle-flies ; it varies much in colour. The female is quite different, being emerald-green.

Agrion splendens (Plate **10**, *2*). Attains 32 mm. (1¼ in.). Common from the Midlands to the South, and in most of Wales and Ireland. Absent from Scotland. Imago (the Banded Agrion) most common in June and July. As in the case of *A. virgo*, the male of this species (Plate **6**, *3*) differs much in colour from the female (Plate **6**, *4*).

Lestes sponsa (Plate **10**, *3*). Attains 26 mm. (1 in.). Among vegetation of ponds and ditches, also in brackish water. It is common, although rare in the Home Counties and in the Midlands. Imago commonest in August.

Pyrrhosoma nymphula (Plate **10**, *4*). Attains 19 mm. (¾ in.). Found in quiet waters on sunken leaves, also in brackish water. Very common. Imago (Plate **8**, *2*, female) is on the wing from May to July.

Ischnura elegans (Plate **10**, *5*). Attains 20 mm. (¾ in.). On vegetation in slow-moving waters. Exceedingly common. Imago (the Common Ischnura) is on the wing from May to August ; it is very slender, and dark greenish-black in colour.

Enallagma cyathigerum (Plate **10**, *6*). Attains 20 mm. (¾ in.). Very common on water-weeds. Bright green in colour, occasionally brown. Imago (Plate **6**, *2*, male) seen in June, July and August.

Nymphs of Dragonflies (sub-order *ANISOPTERA*)

Cordulegaster boltonii (Plate **10**, *7*). Attains 41 mm. (1⅝ in.). Under the debris of rapid-moving water, sometimes in mud. Only common locally, mostly in the West, South of Scotland, and in the southern counties. Imago seen from the end of June to the beginning of September. The Dragonfly has circles of black and yellow bands, and is one of our largest species.

Brachytron pratense (Plate **10**, *8*). Attains 40 mm. (1 9/16 in.). Mainly in England and Wales, in ponds, etc., on sticks and debris to which it holds closely. Imago (Plate **9**, *3*, male) is on the wing from May to the middle of July. Colour of female dark brown.

Anax imperator (Plate **10**, *9*). Attains 54 mm. (2⅛ in.). Most waters, especially among reeds, but common only in the south-eastern counties. Absent from Scotland, doubtful in Ireland.

Imago (the Emperor Dragonfly) is seen especially in June and July. This is one of our three largest species, and in appearance resembles those of the genus *Aeshna* (see following).

Aeshna cyanea (Plate **12**, *1*). Attains 48 mm. (1⅞ in.). Very common in the southern counties on weeds in still waters. Absent from Scotland and Ireland. Imago (Plate **8**, *4*, male) is seen from summer to autumn, especially July and August.

Aeshna juncea (Plate **12**, *2*). Attains 43 mm. (1 11/16 in.). Common on weeds in ponds, also peat pools in mountains. The adult (Plate **8**, *3*—male) attacks other Dragonflies and Demoiselles, in addition to other insects. Common from the end of July and during August. Its colour varies with age and sex.

Aeshna grandis (Plate **12**, *3*). Attains 43 mm. (1 11/16 in.). Common only in midland and southern counties, on pond weeds. Imago seen towards the end of July and in August. The Dragonfly is entirely brown in colour. It flies until dark.

Cordulia aenea (Plate **12**, *4*). Attains 22 mm. (⅞ in.). Conceals itself among debris in slow-moving waters where there are reeds and rushes. Imago emerges in June. It is bronze-green in colour, eyes brilliant emerald-green.

Orthetrum coerulescens (Plate **12**, *5*). Attains 19 mm. (¾ in.). Especially in pools on moors, chiefly in southern counties, but recorded as far north as Inverness; fairly common in Ireland. The imago is blue in colour and emerges chiefly in July and August.

Libellula quadrimaculata (Plate **12**, *6*). Attains 26 mm. (1 in.). Very common locally on the debris at the bottom of pools. Imago (Plate **9**, *4*, male) is on the wing in spring and early summer, particularly in June and July. Its numbers are increased by immigrants. Variable in size and colouring.

Libellula depressa (Plate **12**, 7). Attains 25 mm. (1 in.). Very common in the southern counties, absent from North-west England, Scotland and Ireland. Lives in the mud and debris of ditches, ponds and lakes. Imago (Plate **9**, *1*—male; *2*—female) is seen especially in June and July. Colour variable with age and sex.

Sympetrum striolatum (Plate **12**, *8*). Attains 18 mm. (¾ in.). Common in mud and weeds of ponds. Imago (Plate **6**, *1*, male) is on the wing in late summer and autumn. It is chiefly red and yellow-brown, or the red may be absent.

Sympetrum scoticum (Plate **12**, 9). Attains 15 mm. (⁹⁄₁₆ in.). Common in lakes and boggy ponds having reeds and rushes, particularly in Scotland. The species is more common where there are moors and marshes.

Order THYSANOPTERA. *Thrips*

Description. Minute insects. Body slender, length 1 to 3 mm. Piercing mouth-parts. Antennae 6- to 9-jointed. Wingless or with very narrow wings fringed with hairs. Metamorphosis incomplete. Colour mostly black or yellow.

Classification. Two sub-orders, the TEREBRANTIA, having a saw-like ovipositor and at least one longitudinal vein in the fore wings, and the TUBULIFERA, having no ovipositor and hardly any venation in the wings. (About 183 British species.)

Thrips or Thunder Flies live on flowers, among foliage, in decaying plants, wood and fungi. Some

45

are predatory in habit and attack Aphids, but the majority of them feed on plants, and because of their numbers they can become serious economic pests. The worst of these are the Onion Thrips, the Turnip Thrips and the Bean Thrips. Other Thrip pests attack pears, grasses, etc., and infest greenhouses. Many species are not particular what they feed upon.

In some species males are rare and eggs are able to develop parthenogenetically (= unfertilized by the male).

Order HEMIPTERA. *True Bugs.*

Description. Usually with four wings, the fore pair mostly modified to a horny consistency; the hind pair membranous and transparent. Mouth-parts adapted for piercing and sucking. Metamorphosis gradual, rarely complete. Colour, great variety.

Classification. Two sub-orders, the HETEROPTERA, having the fore wings horny and the hind wings transparent, the wings generally overlap each other over the abdomen; and the HOMOPTERA, in which the four wings are transparent and usually sloping over the sides of the body. Metamorphosis incomplete, or complete in males and incomplete in females.

The HOMOPTERA are further divided into two series, (i) the *Auchenorrhyncha*, and (ii) the *Sternorrhyncha*.

There is also a further division of the HETEROPTERA which it is useful to note. They may, for convenience, be divided into two series of species, (i) the *Gymnocerata*, the Land Bugs (pages 47-49), having the antennae conspicuous, and (ii) the *Cryptocerata*, the Water Bugs (pages 50-51), antennae concealed. (Over 1,411 British species.)

A marked characteristic of this order is that all species, animal and vegetable feeders alike, live by piercing and sucking at all stages of their lives. They have for this a specially developed beak (*rostrum*), which is held below against the body when not in use. The proboscis or beak consists of a sheath containing four piercers needed for making an opening into which the rostrum proper is pushed for sucking out the plant-juices, or blood in the case of a small number of carnivorous species. Bugs are also called " Rhynchota " (*rhynchos*, proboscis), after the specialized mouth structure.

Habits of HETEROPTERA. Whilst the eggs of the sub-order Homoptera are in general fairly simple in structure and ovoid in shape, those of the Heteroptera are, on the contrary, objects of much beauty as regards shape, sculpture and colouring. However, despite the diversity, they are constant in the different families, and may act as a guide to identification. There are also curious structural peculiarities on some eggs, such as filaments, a fringe of processes encircling an operculum (egg-cap) and so on.

From the egg emerges a nymph which develops, by gradual changes, into the adult. The insects may therefore be met at all stages of development, and some diversity of structure and colouring may bring about some confusion in identification. This may be seen from the examples illustrated. *Pyrrhocoris apterus* (Plate **11**, *6*), the only British member of the family Pyrrhocoridae, the Red Bugs, is shown beside its nymph (Plate **11**, *7*) : the latter on attaining a length of 10 mm. moults into its final form. A comparison between the imago of *Gastrodes grossipes* (Plate **11**, *4*) and its nymph (Plate **11**, *5*) illustrates a stage in the metamorphosis of a very common species. It lives chiefly on Scotch Pine, the adults being found from

47

the beginning of July to the beginning of August. The range in difference between the first and last (the fifth) instars of a nymph is shown in that of *Acanthosoma haemorrhoidale* (Plate **14**, *1* shows the first instar, the fifth is shown at *2*). This species, found on Hawthorn and other trees from August to October, belongs to the family Pentatomidae, the Shield Bugs. The members of this family of the Heteroptera are noted for their beauty of colouring. They are also most interesting for the way in which they care for their young, as in the common *Elasmostethus interstinctus* (Plate **11**, *2*) which lives mainly on Birch trees, as well as on other common British trees. The adult insect appears in August. One of the commonest Shield Bugs is *Piezodorus lituratus* (Plate **11**, *1*), found on Furze, where the whole of its life seems to be spent. *Coreus marginatus* belongs to the family Coreidae, Shield Bugs, which are narrower in shape than the related family of Pentatomidae, and which are able to emit more nauseous and penetrating odours than their close relations.

Many Bugs are slender in shape. Such is the very common species *Phytocoris ulmi* (Plate **11**, *8*), of the family Miridae, the adults being found from June to October on plants and trees. Other examples are *Calocoris ochromelas* (Plate **11**, *9*), very common on Oak from April to July, and *Dicyphus epilobii* (Plate **13**, *1*) found from July to October, and even later, on *Epilobium hirsutum*, (the Great Willow Herb). It is a Bug which appears to be more widely distributed here than abroad. *Cyllecoris histrionicus* (Plate **13**, *2*) is also widely distributed, and found on Oak from the middle of June to July, occasionally in August. It varies in colour. *Orthotylus ericetorum* (Plate **13**, *3*) belongs to a genus of green Bugs which escape notice because of the colour and small size, the largest measuring only 6·5 mm. ($\frac{1}{4}$ in.). This insect is, however, common from July to October on *Calluna vulgaris* (Ling) and species of *Erica* (Heaths). The common *Harpocera thoracica* (Plate **13**, 4) is found on Hawthorn, Oak, Birch, Hazel and Sallow, from late May to June; it has distinctive antennae. Later, from June to August, we shall find *Phylus pallipes* (Plate **13**, 5) on Oak, as well as the closely related *P. melanocephalus*. *Psallus variabilis* (Plate **13**, 6) varies much in colour, and is found from June to July on Sallow and Aspen. Not common.

The familiar insects known as Pond Skaters are Bugs of the family Hydrometridae. The most noteworthy of them is *Hydrometra stagnorum* (Plate **14**, 4) which walks in a leisurely manner over the surface of stagnant water and—like others of its kind—cannot get wet due to its light weight and its covering of fine hairs. *Gerris gibbifer* (Plate **14**, 3) is another member of the family, but has the rapid habits of the other species, and jumps along the surface. Pond Skaters feed mainly on dead insects. Some species are wingless.

The Reduviidae, the Assassin Bugs (including the Nabidae), form a very extensive family of aggressive carnivores. *Empicoris vagabundus* (Plate **14**, 5) hunts its living prey on the trunks of trees and Furze, from July to October. From May to October *Reduvius personatus* (Plate **14**, 6) can be found. It is nocturnal and also frequents houses, where it attacks, among other insects, *Cimex lectularius* (Plate **14**, 7), the Bed Bug, of the family Cimicidae. The latter is a pest of dirty houses: it lives behind wallpaper, in cracks, etc., and comes out in the dark to feed on blood from the exposed parts of the skin of sleeping people. The fore wings of all *Cimex* species have degenerated into mere pads, and there is no trace of a hind pair.

CRYPTOCERATA, *The Water Bugs*

(Order HEMIPTERA, sub-order *HETEROPTERA*)

The Water Bugs have their antennae hidden, a feature which gave rise to the name *CRYPTO-CERATA*, Hidden Horns. In addition to the fact that Water Bugs are normally found in water, the apparent absence of antennae helps to identify them readily, especially as they differ in shape among themselves: see Plate **15**, all are *CRYPTOCERATA*, as well as *7* and *8* on Plate **13**, where is also shown the marked difference between Water Bugs and Land Bugs (*1* to *6*). The latter are *GYMNOCERATA*, with antennae always very evident. The absence of antennae also immediately separates them from most Water Beetles (Order COLEOPTERA), whose antennae are visible with the exception of those of Whirligig Beetles (family *Gyrinidae*, page 83).

The Water Bugs may be found in all stretches of water not chemically polluted by factories and the like, and quite stagnant water in the countryside and even in towns may be visited by them. They live submerged, and are not to be found on the surface, like Pond Skaters, who belong to the antennae-visible group of Gymnocerata (Plate **14**, *3* and *4*). Water Bugs occasionally fly from pond to pond. The eggs are laid on vegetation in water from which the young emerge and develop gradually into the adult form.

Ilyocoris (=*Naucoris*) *cimicoides* (Plate **15**, *2*), of the family Naucoridae, is quite a large and common insect of still waters, where it lives among the weeds. Somewhat smaller and brighter in colour is *Aphelocheirus aestivalis* (Plate **13**, *7*), a fast swimmer in rivers; perhaps due to this it is not easily found, though it appears to be quite plentiful when discovered. A most extraordinary water-dweller is *Ranatra linearis* (Plate **15**, *4*, nat. size), a Water Scorpion (family Nepidae), whose first pair of legs are modified for seizing prey, and are quite useless for walking, so that this insect appears to have only four legs. Our other Water Scorpion is *Nepa cinerea* (Plate **15**, *1*). It is the more common of these two British species, and it looks like a dead leaf. The abdominal appendages shown in the illustrations are for breathing, and are not stings. Victims are held by the raptorial fore legs whilst the juices are sucked. The eggs of *Nepa* are laid in chains, and adhere to each other by means of filaments. Many aquatic insects lay their eggs inside plant stems. The female of the common *Notonecta glauca* (Plate **13**, *8*) has an ovipositor or egg-placer for this purpose. Notonectids can inflict painful bites, and are aggressive destroyers of tadpoles, small fish, etc. They are noted for swimming upside down, unlike the related family of Corixidae, such as *Corixa punctata* (Plate **15**,*5*) and *C*. (=*Sigara*) *striata* (Plate **15**, *6*), who do not have this curious Notonectid habit. Their legs are hairy, adapted for swimming, the third pair being particularly powerful and conspicuous, and give the impression of being oars attached to a tiny boat; hence the insects are popularly known as Water Boatmen. Not all species have the legs developed in this manner, however; for instance the small Bug *Plea leachi* (Plate **15**, *3*), only crawls slowly about duckweed and other vegetation.

Sub-order HOMOPTERA
(Order HEMIPTERA)

The important anatomical feature of this sub-order is that its members have four transparent wings (cf. page 46). These insects are diverse in structure, and include the families

Cicadidae—Cicadas, *Cercopidae*—Froghoppers or Cuckoo-spit insects, *Membracidae*—Tree-hoppers, *Jassidae* (*Cicadellidae*)—Leafhoppers; all are included in the series *AUCHENOR-RHYNCHA*. The second series of this sub-order are the *STERNORRHYNCHA*, including the many species of the gardener's plant pests, such as the *Psyllidae*—Jumping Plant-lice, *Aleyrodidae*—White-flies, *Aphididae*—Green-fly, *Coccidae*—Scale-insects, Mealy-bugs.

We have all heard of the Cicadas of the South of France, and of Fabre's complaints about the noise of the males. Joubert has summed up our thoughts about them: "Sunshine and summer heat, without the accompaniment of the Cicada's song, or the quivering of the air, is like a dance without music." Nevertheless we have in the British Isles one species that does not appear to mind our climate. It is *Cicadetta montana*, but it is found only in the New Forest; its larvae feed on the roots and on the stems of bracken.

Cuckoo-spit found on plants is a protective froth made by the nymphs of the broad-headed family, Cercopidae, the commonest being *Philaenus leucophthalmus*. *Cercopis vulnerata* (Plate **13**, 9) is a uniquely coloured native Froghopper, found in some districts on Alder and Sallow. Leafhoppers (family Jassidae) are extremely common and when disturbed will leap several feet, or fly away.

The most numerous individuals on plants and trees are Plant-lice, Green-fly, White-fly, Aphids, Scale-insects and Mealy-bugs. These are the insects whose progeny would soon turn the world into an uninhabitable waste were it not for the havoc wrought on them by the weather, birds, etc., but most of all by other insects, both parasites and predators. A curious feature about them is that they discharge continuously a sugary waste known

52

as honey-dew. This is highly attractive to Ants, who, in order to procure it, make regular journeys to plants and up trees infested with these redoubtable pests ; it is also very attractive to many night-flying Moths.

Plant-lice and Aphids have winged and wingless forms, and they live mainly on new shoots. They are remarkable for their different methods of development, for within one species they will be found to lay eggs and also to be viviparous, whilst the non-fertilization of females by males also obtains, and indeed males are often very rare in certain generations. Structure, food-plants and habits may also change from one generation to another, constituting a regular but complex series of events. One species, for example, after over-wintering as eggs laid in the autumn by sexual females, will produce wingless females which hatch from the eggs in spring, and are viviparous and parthenogenetic (= no fertilization by the male necessary for fertility). From their eggs come similar females, but some are now winged, and these may fly away to infest other plants. This succession goes on during the whole season until the end of the summer or into the autumn, when sexual males and females occur, these females being once again fertilized egg-layers, so that the cycle is now complete. There are also migratory species who must change food-plants according to seasonal availability. A foreign species, *Phylloxera quercus*, has twenty-one forms !

The following are a few of the many common garden and nursery pests comprised in the three families of Sternorrhyncha mentioned on page 52.

The common pest of greenhouses is the Greenhouse White-fly, *Trialeurodes vaporariorum*, of the family Aleyrodidae. It is also known as the Ghost Fly. The species attacks anything growing under glass, and particularly tomatoes. The insect is a foreign immigrant which is unable to live the whole year round out-of-doors.

An all-too-common representative of the family Psyllidae (or Chermidae) is the Apple Sucker, *Chermes mali*, the nymph of which is very injurious to Apple blossom. Species of Aphides are also exceedingly common, such as *Eriosoma lanigerum*, the notorious Woolly Aphis, also known as American Blight. It produces the white wool-like masses of sticky material found on fruit-trees. The Bean Aphis is *Doralis* (=*Aphis*) *rumicis*, also called Black Aphis, Black Blight, etc.

The Scale-insects are comprised in the family Coccidae. The Brown Scale is *Eulecanium corni*, which is common on fruit bushes and wild plants. The Mussel Scale is *Lepidosaphes ulmi*, the commonest of all Scale Insects, being particularly abundant in Apple orchards. Its popular name is derived from its scales, which resemble miniature mussels.

The life-histories of pests belonging to other genera are similarly all extremely interesting to read about, and will be found explained in larger textbooks. Their complex lives require volumes to themselves; the remedy against them has been pointed out by " C. H. P." in *The Countryman*:

Weep not for little greenflies who are orphaned in the morning;
They need no mother's tender care—by evening they'll be spawning.
Nor doth the greenfly malice bear for swatting her relations!
She just lays eggs upon the dregs of slaughtered generations.
And if she comes up smiling when with soap-suds she's been plastered,
      There's only one thing to be done,
      So let me go and get my gun,
      And shoot the little dastard!

THE SUB-CLASS *PTERYGOTA* (continued)
Division (b), *ENDOPTERYGOTA*

The most highly evolved insects belong to the *ENDOPTERYGOTA* (cf. page 23). Their larvae reveal no external evidence of the future winged insects into which they will eventually be transformed.

The complete metamorphosis undergone by these insects—from egg, larva, pupa to the adult winged form—is one of the most spectacular marvels of the animal kingdom. Much remains to be learned of the life-histories of these and other insects; the scope for further pioneer study remains as limitless as ever.

Order NEUROPTERA. *Alderflies, Snakeflies, Lacewings*

Description. Body soft. Antennae long. Mouth-parts adapted for biting. Four similar membranous wings, held roof-wise when at rest. Larvae carnivorous with mouth-parts adapted for biting or sucking. Includes aquatic larvae.

Classification. Two sub-orders, the MEGA-LOPTERA, Alderflies and Snakeflies, usually having no marked bifurcation of the branches of the veins near the margins of the wings, larvae with biting mouth-parts; and the PLANIPENNIA, Lacewings, etc., usually having the branches of the veins markedly bifurcated at the margins of the wings, larvae with mouth-parts adapted for sucking. (60 British species.)

This order comprises weak-flying insects. They possess much diversity of form, and their life-histories are just as varied. Individuals are not found in large numbers, but they are by no means uncommon. The larvae, all carnivorous feeders, are particularly curious in structure, especially so in the case of the aquatic forms.

Sub-order MEGALOPTERA. *Alderflies and Snake-flies* (Order NEUROPTERA)

It has been suggested that Alderflies and Snake-flies should be separated into two distinct orders because these insects differ in many respects from each other. The reasons are of no concern to us here, where we need but consider a few of the common species. Alderflies (family Sialidae), such as *Sialis lutaria* (Plate **16**, " set "—*4*, at rest—*5*), lay their eggs upon plants and objects close to the edge of water. One female will lay as many as 200 to 700 greyish eggs, kept together in one mass. On hatching, the larvae make their way to the water, where they may be found in the mud of ponds and slow-moving streams. The larvae are carnivorous and have well-developed jaws for seizing other larvae, worms, and so on. They have complicated lateral processes, often jointed, attached to the abdominal segments ; these are breathing gills. The larva of *Sialis lutaria* with these processes is shown on Plate **16**, *6*. The larvae leave the water when fully grown and burrow into the soil, where they pupate.

The Snakeflies, family Raphidiidae, with three British species, are found in woods, on Hawthorn when in blossom, and other flowers. They are, however, not common. *Raphidia notata* (Plate **5**, *6*) is illustrated as an example of the unusual appearance of these insects, making them easily recognizable and demonstrating the origin—as in the case of Scorpion-flies—of their popular English name. The eggs are inserted by means of an ovipositor into openings in bark. The larvae live mainly under loose bark ; they are very voracious predators of soft-bodied insects.

Pl. 21 LEPIDOPTERA: WOODLAND BUTTERFLIES D 57

1. Silver-washed Fritillary, male. 2 and 3. Pearl-bordered Fritillary, male and female. (*All natural size.*) *Pages 66–68.*

Pl. 22   LEPIDOPTERA :   CATERPILLARS

Above, left : Cream-spot Tiger Moth.   *Above, right :*
Pine Hawk Moth.   *Below :* Lobster Moth. (*All
natural size.*)   *Pages* 71, 73, 7⁶.

Pl. 23

LEPIDOPTERA :
HEATH AND HILLSIDE BUTTERFLIES

1 and 2. Small Copper, male and female. 3. Adonis
Blue, male. 4. Chalkhill Blue, male. 5 and 6.
Common Blue, female and male. (*All natural size.*)
Pages 68–70.

Pl. 24 LEPIDOPTERA : CATERPILLARS

Above : Silver-washed Fritillary. *Centre :* Old Lady Moth. *Below :* Emperor Moth. (*All natural size.*) Pages 67, 74, 78.

Pl. 25   LEPIDOPTERA :   MIGRANT BUTTERFLIES

1. Red Admiral, male.   2 and 3. Clouded Yellow, male
and female.   4. Painted Lady, male.   (*All natural
size.*)   *Pages* 70–71.

Pl. 26.   LEPIDOPTERA

Above : Angle Shades Moth ($\times$ 2), *p.* 18. *Below* :
Chrysalis of Orange-tip Butterfly ($\times$ 2½), *p.* 63.

Pl. 27

Left: Lobster Moth (*natural size*). Right: Old Lady Moth, female (*slightly reduced*). Pages 17, 76, 78.

LEPIDOPTERA

Pl. 28   LEPIDOPTERA : HAWK MOTHS

1. Lime Hawk, male. 2. Eyed Hawk, male. 3.
Elephant Hawk, male. 4. Humming-bird Hawk,
male. (*All natural size.*) *Pages* 71–73.

Pl. 29   LEPIDOPTERA

Above : Caterpillar of the Pebble Prominent Moth
(× 1¼). *Below :* Lappet Moth (*natural size*). **Pages**
17, 76.

Pl. 30   LEPIDOPTERA : TIGER MOTHS AND
                    DAY-FLYERS

1. Garden Tiger, male. 2. Cream-spot Tiger, male.
3. Emperor, male. 4. Cinnabar, male. 5. Six-spot
Burnet, male. (*All natural size.*) *Pages* 73–75.

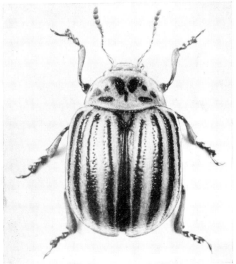

Pl. 31   COLEOPTERA : BEETLES

Above: A Carrion Beetle, *Oeceoptoma thoracicum* (13 to 16 mm., $\frac{1}{2}$ to $\frac{5}{8}$ in.).   *Below :* Colorado Beetle, *Leptinotarsa decemlineata* (11 mm., $\frac{7}{16}$ in.).   Pages 87, 89.

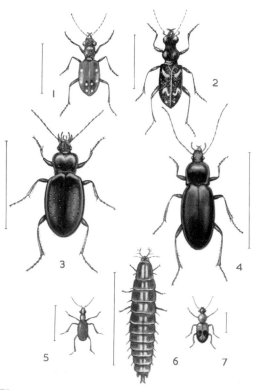

Pl. 32   COLEOPTERA: BEETLES

1. Tiger Beetle, *Cicindella campestris*. 2. *C. sylvatica*.
3. *Carabus nemoralis*. 4. *C. violaceus*. 5. Bombardier
Beetle, *Brachinus crepitans*. 6. Carabid larva. 7.
Badister bipustulatus. *Pages 82–83.*

Sub-order PLANIPENNIA. *Lacewings*, etc.
(Order NEUROPTERA)

Varied as this group of insects is, their larvae nevertheless bear a greater resemblance to each other than do the adult insects, these—especially foreign species—being often very different in form. All larvae have piercing and sucking mouth-parts, and are carnivorous feeders.

British species, however, may be referred to as Lacewings, so named after their relatively large, transparent, gauze-like wings, which are held roof-wise over the body when at rest. Large wings, in relation to the size of the body, are rarely attributes of fast fliers, and indeed the flight of Lacewings is a leisurely, gentle business which would be a highly dangerous undertaking if they were not crepuscular and nocturnal in habit.

The commonest of these insects are the Green Lacewings (family Chrysopidae), especially *Chrysopa carnea* (Plate **16**, " set "—*3*, at rest—*2*), which comes inside houses and other buildings to hibernate. This species is remarkable in that it loses its green colour during the over-wintering period, when it is reddish, but it regains its characteristic pale green in the spring. The eggs are attached to the underside of leaves and are borne on stalk-like threads, so that they are protectively raised away from the leaf. Photographs of a Lacewing and of eggs are shown on Plate **17**. Lacewing larvae have the features of larval predators, well-developed eyes, useful jaws, and legs that give them freedom of movement. They feed especially on Plant-lice of all kinds, and are most helpful to gardeners. Some species attach debris to their bodies. When ready to pupate, the larvae spin hard cocoons of white silk on leaves and other suitable supports. Unlike most insect larvae, they produce their silk in transformed abdominal organs

57

(Malpighian tubes), and it comes out of an anal spinneret.

The adults are sometimes known as Golden Eyes, from the bright lustre to be seen in their large compound eyes. Other species are also called Stink-flies because when handled they are able to emit a disagreeable smell from glands situated in the thorax.

There are also smaller species of sombre colour known as Brown Lacewings (family Hemerobiidae). They are much more delicate in appearance than the Green Lacewings, and they do not raise their eggs from the surface to which they are attached. The larvae also feed on Aphids.

The largest member of this order of Neuroptera belongs to the family Osmylidae; it is *Osmylus fulvicephalus* (Plate **16**, *1*, with wings " set "), found from May to July in dense vegetation beside clear streams. This species, too, does not raise its eggs on stalks. The larvae hatch about July and are amphibious. They live in mosses, and will go into water in search of small larvae, particularly those of Flies. Pupation, in cocoons, takes place in April and May.

Order MECOPTERA. *Scorpion-flies*

Description. Slender carnivorous insects. Head beak-like. Antennae long and thin. Long, slender legs. Four similar membranous wings, held lengthwise and horizontally when at rest. Larvae carnivorous, having three pairs of thoracic legs. Metamorphosis complete.

Classification. A well-defined order divided into families with three hundred species. (4 British species.)

The popular name for this insect is derived from the easily recognized male, which has the last abdominal segments curved upwards (Plate **5**, *5*);

it reminds one of a scorpion. Another very distinctive feature is the beak-like head, such as that of *Panorpa communis* (Plate **16**, 7), which greatly helps in the identification of these insects. They are carnivorous at all stages of their lives, but they seem to prefer dead or injured insects. Scorpion-flies live in shady and damp vegetation. The caterpillar-like larvae pupate in the soil. The pupa is capable of movement when disturbed, and apparently makes its way to the surface when the adult is about to emerge.

Order TRICHOPTERA. *Caddisflies*

Description. Moth-like insects. Mouth-parts vestigial or absent. Antennae bristly. Wings membranous and hairy, held roof-wise when at rest. Much venation but few cross-veins. Larvae aquatic, usually living in cases.

Classification. The order is divided into families only. (188 British species.)

Superficially these insects resemble dull-coloured moths, but instead of having a scaly covering, their wings and bodies are clothed in dense hairs. The mouth-parts are not adapted for sucking, but they can sip fluids, and when at rest the adult insects fold the wings like a roof over their backs. The eggs are laid in or near water and are surrounded by a gelatinous covering. The larvae are aquatic and breathe with gills. As a protection for their soft bodies they construct cases of various materials around themselves and move about by protruding their harder fore parts and legs. The pupae or nymphs are mobile and can bite their way out of the cases when the imagines are due to emerge.

Caddisflies are almost invariably found near still, fresh water or by streams. Most of them rest quietly during the day, hidden in the herbage or on tree-trunks, and begin to fly at dusk. They often enter houses, flying to the light, and will also come to feed from sweet liquids. Their flight is generally rather feeble and the soft wings are dark in colour. The largest British species, *Phryganea grandis* (Plate **18**, *1*), has a wing-span of just over two inches. The antennae are long and the fore wings brown with lighter blotches and the hind wings a uniform smoky colour. The small green eggs are laid in batches of up to 700, enveloped in a broad band of jelly. This is attached in a loop to the underside of some floating leaf. The larvae (Plate **18**, *2*) hatch in about ten days, and at once cover their soft hind bodies by cases built of silk to which are fixed short pieces cut from the stems of water-plants, or even algae. These pieces are all of equal length and are arranged in a regular spiral pattern. The full-grown larva is one and a half inches long, carries tufts of gills all the way down its body and has a sharp-pointed spine on the last segment of the thorax. Before pupating it burrows down into the mud near the shore of the lake or pond and closes the entrance to the case, leaving only just enough space to allow for fresh water to seep through. When the time for emerging is near, the pupa or nymph burrows out of this case and swims to some suitable reed or water-plant, so that it can then crawl up to the surface before the pupal skin splits and the imago comes out and dries its wings.

Many different materials are used by the Caddis larvae in the construction of their cases. Those living in still waters make their cases as light as possible to facilitate movement, whilst those in running water tend to make use of heavier material, such as sand or tiny stones, which will act as ballast. Some of the Caddis-worms living in swift-flowing streams, however, make no cases at all, and either live under stones or construct silken tunnels in which they hide. These tunnels always face upstream and have wide funnel-shaped openings which act as traps, catching various small insects and floating plants which serve as food for the larvae. Only when about to pupate do these free Caddis larvae construct protective cases, inside which they spin a silken cocoon. Most Caddis larvae hold on to their cases with two curved spines on the last segment of the body, and their grip is so firm that it is almost impossible to pull them out of their cases without injuring them. The best method of removing a larva from its case is by slitting the case carefully with a razor blade. A denuded Caddis larva will make itself a new case in little more than an hour, incorporating any material which may happen to be at hand.

The majority of the Caddis-worms are vegetarian, feeding on diatoms, algae and water-plants, but there are also a few carnivorous species. Most of them crawl about on the submerged vegetation, or on the bottom of the ponds and streams, but a few build fixed cases, particularly if they live in fast-flowing streams. They sometimes cluster together in groups. A few species are not truly aquatic in habit but spend their larval period amongst the damp moss around springs or in wet leaves and herbage. In one species the female insect is unable to fly, as the wings are only rudimentary.

The order of Trichoptera is divided into seven families, but identification of adult Caddisflies is very difficult. The cases of the worms are a good aid to the beginner, as they differ very much in shape and construction. A good plan is to collect the worms and breed them out in captivity, keeping the species separate to avoid confusion.

Order LEPIDOPTERA. *Butterflies and Moths*

Description. Four membranous wings. Few cross-veins. Body, wings and appendages covered with broad scales. Principal mouth-parts generally a suctorial proboscis formed by the maxillae. Metamorphosis complete. Some larvae possess eight pairs of limbs.

Classification. It has been the custom to divide the LEPIDOPTERA into *RHOPALOCERA* (Butterflies, in the British species always with clubbed antennae) and *HETEROCERA* (Moths, antennae very varied). There are, however, objections to such divisions, as there are also objections to the familiar amateur divisions of *MACRO-* and *MICROLEPIDOPTERA*, based on size criteria. Scientifically the LEPIDOPTERA are classed in two sub-orders, the *HOMONEURA*, having the venation of the fore and hind wings almost identical, and the *HETERONEURA*, with venation of fore and hind wings markedly different. The *HETERONEURA* comprise a large assembly of species divided into superfamilies and families. (2,187 British species.)

For convenience we here divide the Lepidoptera into two groups, Rhopalocera and Heterocera, generally referred to as Butterflies and Moths. These insects, with the exception of a few wingless female Moths, all have four wings, covered in minute overlapping scales which are easily rubbed off. All Butterflies, and most Moths, have mouth-parts in the shape of a long tongue, adapted for sucking nectar from flowers, but a few Moths are unable to feed at all in the imago stage.

The main distinction between British Butterflies and Moths lies in the antennae. In Butterflies these organs are narrow with a club-shaped tip. In Moths they vary very much and are sometimes large and feathery, sometimes thin and thread-like, rarely clubbed, the Burnets * being the one exception.

A typical Butterfly or Moth caterpillar has eight pairs of legs, three jointed pairs with small claws on the thorax or fore body and five pairs of short fleshy abdominal feet which are used for grasping the food-plant on which it sits.

Butterfly chrysalises (pupae) vary greatly in shape and colour, and are sometimes covered with sharp spines. They are frequently attached to a support by a small pad of silk and a silken girdle—such as that of the Orange-tip (Plate **26**)—but are never enclosed in a cocoon. The pupae of Moths are usually brown in colour, fairly smooth and protected by some kind of cocoon made from particles of soil, chewed wood or debris bound together with silk. Sometimes the pupa lies in a chamber hollowed out in the earth.

RHOPALOCERA. *Butterflies*

Butterflies of the Fields and Lanes

In April, Butterflies, which have spent the winter as hibernating caterpillars or chrysalises, begin to emerge. The first to appear on the wing are usually the Green-veined Whites ; the sexes can be distinguished quite easily, for in the spring brood the males are often without markings on their uppersides or have only one indistinct spot,

* As the English names of the more common Butterflies and Moths are now well known and firmly established, the Latin or scientific names are unnecessary here. The latter are given full prominence in Warne's " Wayside and Woodland " series of books dealing with these insects.

whereas the females have three black spots on their fore wings. Very soon they are joined by the Orange-tips (Plate **18**, *3*, *4*), in which the sexual difference is very marked, for only the males have the brilliant colouring that gives them their name. The female Orange-tip may easily be mistaken at a distance for a Green-veined White, but on close examination it will be seen that the underside markings are quite different. In the Green-veined White the ground colour of the hind wings is yellowish-green, with the veining showing up darkly, whilst in the Orange-tip the effect is of a white ground colour stippled with moss-green. Both these species spend the winter in the chrysalis stage attached by silken girdles to plant-stems (Plate **26**).

The Green Hairstreak may also be found in lanes in May, but more often inhabits the high hedges around sheltered fields. These little Butterflies spend a great deal of their time resting on the green leaves of Hawthorn bushes, where the colouring of their undersides exactly matches the young green foliage. The best way to find them is to tap the boughs with a stick, when they will fly up into the air and twist and turn in an extraordinary aerobatic display.

The Dingy Skipper and the Grizzled Skipper are both Butterflies of the spring which breed in uncultivated pastures and heathland. The former has the peculiar habit of folding its wings down over its body like a Moth. Later in the season two other Skippers, the Large and the Small, may be found in similar country, both feeding on various grasses in the caterpillar stage. Common Blues, too, are often found in rough pastures if their food-plant, the Bird's-foot Trefoil, grows there, but they are rather local insects, often confined to one corner of a field only; they have two broods during the season.

An occasional Brimstone Butterfly (Plate **18**, *5*, *6*), will be seen in this type of locality any time from late March, when they awake from hibernation, and may remain on the wing until June. Both the sulphur males and the pale parchment-coloured females are restless insects and never settle for long. They are always eager to press on in their flight along the hedges, the females searching for scattered Buckthorn bushes on which to lay their eggs. In midsummer the Meadow Browns begin to emerge, fluttering lazily over the tall grasses at haymaking time and in the nearby lanes the Hedge Brown, or Gatekeeper as it is often called, begins to flit along the hedgerows. Both species spend the winter as small hibernating caterpillars, feeding slowly during the spring and emerging from the chrysalis over quite a long period.

Garden Butterflies

Only two of the Butterflies that inhabit our gardens, the Large and Small Whites, are in any way destructive. Both feed on cabbages in their early stages, but the Large White does the most damage, as the female lays her eggs in large batches, whereas the Small White deposits them singly over a wide area. The caterpillars of the Large White are familiar to most people, being pale yellowish-green mottled all over with dark markings, and they feed in colonies. The Small White is almost exactly the same shade of green as a cabbage leaf.

A true garden Butterfly is the Holly Blue (Plate **20**, *3*, *4*). In the spring the females may be seen laying their eggs on young flowering shoots of Holly, but the second brood insects which emerge later in the summer always select the flower-buds of Ivy; this complete change of food-plants is unique amongst the British Butterflies. This

E

species is one of the few Butterflies which pass the winter in the chrysalis stage, the fully fed caterpillar crawling into the Ivy clump and pupating on the under surface of a leaf.

Peacocks and Small Tortoiseshells (Plate **20**, *1*, *2*), are also familiar garden Butterflies, and the food-plant of both species is Stinging Nettle. They first put in an appearance in early spring, soon after awakening from hibernation, and come to feed from the Purple Aubretia and other rockery plants, both species often living well into May. The Small Tortoiseshell is double- and occasionally treble-brooded, but the Peacock produces only one brood in a season. The summer generations of these two colourful Butterflies usually begin to emerge when the Purple Buddleia bushes break into flower, and they may be seen eagerly feeding from the long, scented trusses.

The Comma (Plate **20**, *5*) seldom comes into gardens in the spring, as it prefers the nectar from Sallow and Willow catkins when it first awakens, but the next generation of Butterflies, reared in some nearby woodland or copse, will seek out flowering Michaelmas Daisies and stay in gardens until the first frosts of autumn kill off the flowers. Then they will return to the woods to hibernate in the open under a branch of a tree. With their curiously ragged wings, the colour of decaying leaves, many of them escape the notice of hungry birds during winter.

Woodland Butterflies

The first Butterfly to be seen on the wing in a sunny glade or riding in early spring is the Speckled Wood, flitting along between the sunlit patches and the shadows. At intervals throughout the summer until quite late in the autumn successive broods of these dark speckled Butterflies haunt the woodland pathways, and as the food-plant of their caterpillars is grass, they are often very abundant.

In May the first of the Fritillaries, the Pearl-bordered Fritillary (Plate **21**, *2*, *3*), is on the wing. It seeks out the patches of purple Bugle flowers, and within a week or so it is joined by a very similar Butterfly, the Small Pearl-bordered Fritillary. Examination of the underside markings of both species clearly shows their difference, however, the Small Pearl-bordered Fritillaries having considerably more silver spots and markings, and the ground colour being darker than in the other species. The females of both these common Fritillaries lay their eggs on Violet plants, and spend the winter hibernating as small caterpillars in curled dead leaves.

In July the largest species, the Silver-washed Fritillary (Plate **21**, *1*), may be seen in company with the White Admiral feeding on the Bramble flowers, of which they are both particularly fond. Although the Silver-washed Fritillary caterpillars feed on Violet leaves, the female Butterfly does not lay her eggs upon the plants, but tucks them into crevices in the bark on tree-trunks, particularly Oaks. On hatching, the minute caterpillars retire at once into hibernation, after eating part of their egg-shells. When spring comes they crawl out of their retreats and wander away in search of Violets (Plate **24**).

The High Brown Fritillary also flies in woods during July, and in the heat of the day likes to haunt open clearings where Thistles are in flower. The Heath Fritillary, despite its name, always inhabits woodlands, but is found in any numbers only locally in Kent and Essex during late June and early July.

The Purple Emperor is another very local insect, and as it likes to spend most of its time flying round the topmost branches of tall trees, it is very seldom seen at close quarters.

Purple Hairstreaks are often quite common during July, and a " cloud " of these dark purple Butterflies may sometimes be disturbed if the lower branches of an Oak tree overhanging a woodland pathway should be tapped with a long stick.

By far the commonest Butterfly of the woods, however, is the Ringlet. It is one of the few Butterflies which does not mind rain and will fly even in dull weather. Both the males and females are distinctly marked with bold rings on the under-side, but in certain districts a form occurs where the markings on the hind wings are reduced to small white dots or are even absent altogether.

Heath and Hillside Butterflies

Perhaps the widest variety of Butterflies can be found in this section, for the majority of the Blues breed on chalk or limestone hills and downs, and two Fritillaries, as well as Browns and Skippers, are found on grassy hillsides and heathland. The Small Heath, a little golden-brown and grey insect, is undoubtedly the most widespread Butterfly in the British Isles, and occurs wherever there is uncultivated grass land, except in the Orkney and Shetland Isles. The caterpillars which hatch from eggs laid in the early summer do not all feed up at the same speed ; some go ahead and produce an autumn brood of Butterflies, while others hibernate through the winter and emerge in the spring ; thus the Butter-fly is on the wing for a long period. The Small Copper (Plate **23**, *1*, *2*) is about the same size and appears at the same time. It flies in open fields in May, July and September, where Sorrel grows, for this is the food-plant of the caterpillars.

The common Wall Brown likes to bask on warm, dry ground with wings spread flat against the earth, while the Grayling, which is much more local and found on rough moorland and on steep granite cliffs sloping to the sea, rests with wings closed on lichen-covered rocks, where the markings on the underside of the hind wings provide a perfect camouflage. The Marbled White, a Brown despite its name, is also local, but often occurs in very large numbers where it breeds. There are colonies in certain woodland clearings in Southern England, on grassy hillsides and cliff-tops by the sea. The females drop their eggs quite casually amongst the grass and herbage as they fly along.

The Dark Green Fritillary, which appears in late July or early August, lives on windswept hills and in wild moorland country, and is the fastest-flying Butterfly in Britain. Earlier in the season, in late May and early June, the Marsh Fritillary is on the wing, and as well as in marshy districts may sometimes be found breeding on grassy hillsides.

Often several species of the Blues can be seen flying together on the chalk downs of Southern England. The first brood of the Adonis Blue (Plate **23**, *3*) emerges at the same time as the Common Blue (Plate **23**, *5*, *6*), in late May, and in company with them may often be seen the Brown Argus. The majority of the females of these Butterflies are not blue at all, but are coloured in various shades of brown, and this often causes confusion. The Adonis and Common Blue are both double-brooded, and their second emergence often overlaps that of the Chalkhill Blue (Plate **23**, *4*). This pale silvery-blue Butterfly, which is single-brooded only, begins to emerge in mid-July, and is on the wing through most of August. The caterpillars of the Adonis and Chalkhill Blues feed only on Horseshoe Vetch, remain hidden during the day and begin to crawl up just before sunset. It is not uncommon to find the Silver-spotted Skipper flying with the Chalkhill Blue, as it emerges about the same time and often breeds in similar terrain. The Small Blue also likes downland, but prefers sheltered hollows or old chalk pits where weeds and grasses provide food and cover for this small, fragile insect.

Migrant Butterflies

It is now generally recognized that the majority of migrant species which arrive in varying numbers each season come from the Mediterranean region. Several times during the last century vast swarms of Painted Lady Butterflies (Plate **25**, *4*) have been seen leaving the African coastal districts and flying northwards, but the reasons for these flights are not yet properly understood. In France the caterpillars of this Butterfly are often a pest on Globe Artichokes, but in this country the green eggs are laid on Thistles.

The Red Admiral (Plate **25**, *1*) never comes in such large numbers as the Painted Lady, but we may be glad that these black-and-scarlet Butter-flies do possess in some degree the instinct to migrate so that we may have them here to grace our gardens. They breed in England every year, brood succeeding brood on Stinging Nettles, but the caterpillars and chrysalids cannot survive our winter climate. A few of the Butterflies may live through the winter, but not in sufficient numbers to re-colonize the countryside in spring.

The Clouded Yellow (Plate **25**, *2, 3*) is another regular migrant, and sometimes arrives in such large numbers that entomologists speak of a " Clouded Yellow year ". Soon after arriving here, these Butterflies spread all over the countryside, the females searching out Lucerne and Clover fields, for it is on these plants that they lay their eggs.

HETEROCERA. Moths

Hawk Moths

These can be divided into two groups: those which are native to this country, and the migrant visitors. They are all noted for their rapid powerful flight, and the majority of them can hover in the air much like the Kestrels. The caterpillars with the exception of that of the Small Elephant, have a characteristic curved horn or spine on the last segment, and most of them are tinted in various shades of green. Several of the more common kinds are named after the trees on which the caterpillars feed.

One often finds the Lime Hawk (Plate **28**, *1*) in suburban gardens where Lime trees are planted along a fence or wall, while the Privet Hawk Moth is attracted by hedges of green Privet. The fully fed caterpillar of this, our largest native Hawk Moth, is a most handsome creature. It is bright apple-green, and on each side of the body are seven sloping white stripes edged in front with violet and behind with yellow, while the tail-horn is like black polished ebony on the upper surface and yellow beneath. The Poplar Hawk is common in parks and recreation grounds where these tall trees are planted as a screen, and also occurs generally in the countryside.

The Pine Hawk, at one time confined to Suffolk and Essex and some districts in Dorset and Hampshire, is now widely distributed in the South of England. It is wonderfully camouflaged in the caterpillar stage (Plate **22**) for when small it is striped longitudinally in green and yellow, so that it is almost invisible when feeding on the needles

71

of a Scots Pine, and in the last skin it becomes a dark reddish-brown, to match the bark of the tree.

The Eyed Hawk (Plate **28**, *2*), which gets its name from the eye-like markings on its pink hind wings, often lays its eggs on Apple trees. The Elephant (Plate **28**, *3*) and Small Elephant Hawks both have caterpillars which resemble this animal in the colour of their skins and in the way in which they extend their front segments and wave them to and fro when questing for food, like an elephant reaching out its trunk for a bun. The Broad-bordered and Narrow-bordered Bee Hawks both have furry bodies and markings rather like certain Bumble-bees ; the former frequents woodland glades in May and June, visiting the flowering Rhododendrons for nectar and laying eggs on Honeysuckle, while the latter is more often seen in damp meadows where the Devil's-bit Scabious grows, on which the caterpillar feeds.

Several of the migrant Hawk Moths are well known in this country, and the large Death's Head, with its skull-mark on the back of the thorax and its ability to squeak like a mouse when touched, is undoubtedly the most remarkable of our Moths. The huge yellowish-green and violet-striped caterpillars or the dark brown pupae are sometimes found when potatoes are harvested. The large grey Convolvulus Hawk visits gardens at dusk in the autumn in search of Sweet-tobacco plants, from which it extracts nectar with a tongue three inches long.

The Humming-bird Hawk Moth (Plate **28**, *4*) so closely resembles the exotic little bird after which it has been named that arguments take place every summer as to whether the creature poised before a flower on hardly perceptible wings is really a bird or an insect. It has the unusual habit of flying throughout the day as well as at dusk and after dark. In years when there is a

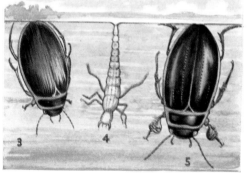

1. Whirligig (family Gyrinidae), usually found only at the surface of the water. Beetles taking air at the surface of the water—2. Great Silver Water Beetle, *Hydrous* (= *Hydrophilus*) *piceus*. *Dytiscus marginalis*— 3. Female ; 4. Larva ; 5. Male. (*All natural size.*) *Pages 82–84.*

Pl. 34   COLEOPTERA : BEETLES

Above : Left, Rhagium bifasciatum (14 to 20 mm., $\frac{9}{16}$ to
$\frac{3}{4}$ *in.*). *Right, Creophilus maxillosus* (19 mm., $\frac{3}{4}$ *in.*).
Below : Left, Necrobia ruficollis (5 mm., $\frac{3}{16}$ *in.*). *Right,
Elater balteatus* (8 mm., $\frac{5}{16}$ *in.*). *Pages* 85–87.

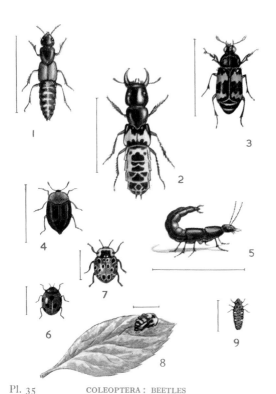

Pl. 35   COLEOPTERA : BEETLES

1. A Rove Beetle, *Staphylinus caesareus*.   2. *Creophilus maxillosus*.   3. A Burying Beetle, *Necrophorus vespillo*. 4. A Carrion Beetle, *Oeceoptoma thoracicum*.   5. Devil's Coach-horse, *Staphylinus olens*.   6. Seven-spot Ladybird, *Coccinella septempunctata*.   7. Eyed Ladybird, *Anatis ocellata*.   8 and 9. Seven-spot Ladybird, pupa and larva.   *Pages* 82, 84, 85, 88, 89.

Pl. 36   COLEOPTERA : BEETLES

Above : Wasp Beetle, *Clytus arietis* (7 to 14 mm., $\frac{5}{16}$ to $\frac{9}{16}$ in.), *pages* 17, 88.   *Below :* Common Cockchafer, *Melolontha melolontha* (26 mm., 1 in.), p. 87.

Pl. 37   COLEOPTERA :
        STAG BEETLES, *Lucanus cervus*

Above : Larva (*slightly enlarged*).   *Below :* Male and
female adults (20 *to* 50 *mm.*, ¾ *to* 2 *in.*).   *Page* 87.

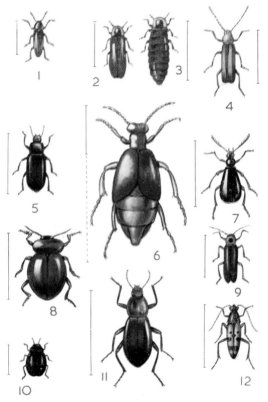

Pl. 38   COLEOPTERA : BEETLES

1. *Agriotes obscurus.*   *Lampyris noctiluca*—2. Male.
3. Wingless female, popularly known as the Glow-worm.   4. *Cantharis abdominalis.*   5. *Tenebrio molitor.*
6. An Oil Beetle, *Meloë proscarabaeus*, varying much in size.   7. *Pyrochroa coccinea.*   8. Bloody-nosed Beetle, *Timarcha tenebricosa.*   9. *Cantharis rustica.*   10. A Leaf Beetle, *Chrysolina staphylaea.*   11. *Blaps mucronata.*   12. *Strangalia maculata.*   *Pages 85–88.*

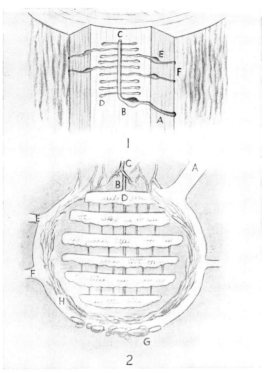

Pl. 39   EXAMPLES OF INSECT ARCHITECTURE

1. A Bark Beetle's home begins with an entrance burrow (*A*), leading to a nuptial chamber (*B*). Eggs are laid along the central gallery (*C*). Each larva makes its own gallery (*D*), a pupal chamber (*E*) and finally an exit burrow (*F*), *p*. 88.   2. The Wasp *Vespula germanica* makes an underground home reached through a tunnel (*A*). An attachment (*B*) is made to a root (*C*) to suspend the combs (*D* is the first). These have a surrounding envelope (*H*). There may also be side galleries (*E* and *F*). Larvae of certain flies are to be found among the detritus at the bottom (*G*), *p*. 99.

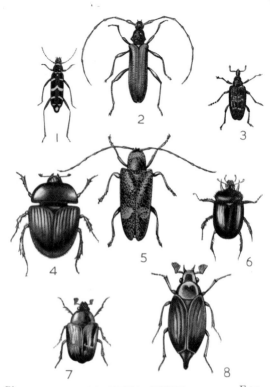

Pl. 40   COLEOPTERA : BEETLES   E 73

1. Wasp Beetle, *Clytus arietis*. 2. Musk Beetle, *Aromia moschata*. 3. *Hylobius abietis*. 4. *Geotrupes stercorarius*. 5. *Saperda carcharias*. 6. A Dung Beetle, *Typhaeus typhoeus*, male. 7. Rose Chafer, *Cetonia aurata*. 8. Common Cockchafer, *Melolontha melolontha*. (*All approx. natural size.*) *Pages* 87–89.

big migration, the caterpillars of this Moth can often be found feeding on Yellow Bedstraw.

Tiger Moths

In the bright Tiger Moths, colours run riot—scarlet, brick-red, orange, yellow, ruby, brown and black, often blotched with white or cream or even dark blue. The caterpillars are all furry, some luxuriantly, others more sparsely, and all move at a surprising speed across the ground. Some of the species have been aptly named after the predominating colour on their wings, but the name Garden Tiger (Plate **30**, *1*) is rather misleading, as this insect is seldom found in gardens, but much more often in country lanes or round the outskirts of farm-yards, feeding on weeds such as Dock, Dandelion and Nettles. The caterpillar is a typical " woolly bear ", chestnut-brown and black with the long, silky hairs tipped with silver.

The Cream-spot Tiger (Plate **30**, *2*) likes similar surroundings, but the caterpillar (Plate **22**) has only short bristly hair growing in tufts all over its dark brown body. The caterpillars of the Scarlet Tiger are quite colourful, mottled in greyish-black and yellow, and may sometimes be found in colonies feeding on Hound's Tongue in damp meadows. The Ruby Tiger is a heath and moorland insect widely distributed all over the British Isles. The Wood Tiger is the only one that really has true tiger colouring, and is attractively striped.

The White and Buff Ermine Moths are also classified as Tigers, and their names describe them well. The caterpillars of both feed on garden weeds, but the White Ermine larva is dark brown, with a reddish stripe along its back, while the Buff Ermine is almost biscuit coloured. Both are bristly rather than silky, and curl up in a ball when touched in true " Tiger " fashion.

Day-flying Moths

Not all Moths fly at night, and it is no wonder, therefore, that some of the brighter day-flying Moths are often confused with Butterflies, especially as there are more Moths on the wing during the day than there are Butterflies on the British List. Some of the Tigers fly in the sunshine, and there are many others. Often before the Birches are in leaf one may see on commons in southern England a number of small Moths spiralling around the upper branches. They are male Orange Underwings performing a courtship flight.

In Scotland, especially at Rannoch and Aviemore, the Kentish Glory Moth behaves in much the same way. The male flies during the afternoon, finds the female and mates with her, but she does not take to the wing until after dusk. Another much more widely distributed Moth is the Emperor (Plate **30**, *3*; caterpillar, Plate **24**), which inhabits wild moorland country in most parts of Britain. On an April day the males can be seen flying low over the heather in a zig-zag course, searching for the large grey females which cling to the stems close to their empty silk cocoons.

In early June the reddish-brown male Fox Moths appear on hills and heaths, and throughout the autumn the large hairy caterpillars can be seen sunning themselves on the slopes—beautiful dark brown creatures with bands of thick velvety-black hair. In July the male Oak Eggars fly during the day in country lanes and on commons. They are rather larger than Fox Moths, but not dissimilar in colouring.

The two common Burnet Moths, the Five- and Six-spot Burnets (Plate **30**, *5*), named after the number of red spots on their glossy blue-black fore wings, fly respectively in May and June and

74

July and August. The former is the more local insect, and both pupate in slug-shaped yellow silken cocoons attached to a grass stem. The Cinnabar (Plate **30**, *4*), another black-and-red Moth, flies both by day and night. The caterpillars, banded in orange and black, are a familiar sight on plants of Ragwort.

One of the commonest day-flying Moths is the small chestnut-brown Vapourer (eggs—Plate **19**). Only the male can fly, as the female is wingless and remains sitting on the silken cocoon. In years when the Silver-Y Moth migrates here in large numbers, this purplish-brown insect, with the prominent silver Y-shaped mark on each fore wing, may become a serious garden pest as the caterpillars feed on many different crops.

A very interesting group of day-flying Moths are the Clearwings. These insects have transparent colourless wings with only a narrow margin of dark scaling round the edges, and their body-colouring is usually in stripes of red, yellow and black. They are a perfect example of mimicry in insects, as they all resemble other insects of the order Hymenoptera. The largest and most striking is the Hornet Clearwing, which to the untrained eye looks exactly like a Hornet. The caterpillars of all species feed inside the twigs, branches or trunks of various shrubs, and the Currant Clearwing is often a pest in Currant plantations, where the burrowing caterpillars cause the death of the twigs or entire bushes. Well pruned bushes are usually more heavily attacked than are neglected ones !

Night-flying Moths

The vast majority of our Moths take to the wing only at dusk. Every species has its set hours of flight, and the experienced collector knows at what time to expect the various Moths to visit sugar-patches or come to artificial light. Moths do not like moonlight nights, and hide away in dark corners during the day.

All the family of Prominents are strongly drawn to light. They take their name from the presence in many species of tufts of hair-like scales projecting from the inner margin of the fore wings. When the Moths close their wings these tufts stand up and are displayed like a fan. Some very familiar Moths are included in this group. The Puss Moth (eggs—Plate 19) and the three species of Kitten Moths all have curious caterpillars, which in their early stages are remarkably like black-and-tan kittens, and later develop purple saddles on their green bodies and huge false eyes, which make a startling impression. The Lobster Moth (Plate 27), too, has an extraordinary caterpillar with the second and third pair of legs so elongated that they give the creature a superficial resemblance to a lobster (Plate 22).

The Buff-tip is well known for its black-and-yellow caterpillars, which feed in colonies on Lime trees in towns and suburbs. The Moth itself looks just like a twig snapped off a Silver Birch, the silvery-grey wings wrapped round its body resembling the bark and the pale yellow areas giving the impression of freshly broken wood.

The Tussock Moths have been well named, for the caterpillars are highly ornamental and often brilliantly coloured, with tufts of hair like miniature shaving-brushes along their backs, usually in vivid contrast to the rest of their colouring. The Vapourer, already mentioned, belongs to this group. Amongst the Eggars the Lackey is the most common. The females lay their eggs in "bracelets" round twigs, and the caterpillars live in a web.

76

The large Lappet (Plate **29**) resembles a crumpled leaf, as the edges of both pairs of wings are sharply dentated; the caterpillars, too, are wonderfully camouflaged as they sit closely pressed to a twig of Blackthorn which their colouring exactly resembles. Another large Moth in the same group is the Drinker, so named after the caterpillar's habit of imbibing drops of dew on the grasses where it feeds.

The Footmen form quite a large group of Moths. With the exception of the Red-necked Footman, which is black with a red collar, they are mostly in shades of cream and yellow.

The largest group among the Moths are the Noctuids, numbering over eighty species. Most of them are dull grey or brown and of small or medium size. Some resemble each other closely, and identification is difficult. The Underwings are an exception, for they have brilliant hind wings, usually banded with black. The best known is the Large Yellow Underwing, often found in garden sheds and summer-houses. When disturbed the Moth will run along like a mouse seeking shelter, instead of taking to the wing. The Red Underwing rests by day on fences and tree-trunks, where it is almost invisible, but the moment it flies the brilliant red underwings are fully exposed.

The Wainscot family number over thirty species, most of them light-coloured insects whose caterpillars feed inside the stems of reed and water-plants and on grasses. The largest of these is the Bulrush Wainscot, whose larvae live in the stems of the familiar reed mace, which is usually referred to as the bulrush. The female has a pair of spines at the tip of her body and with these she can actually cut holes in the reed mace stem in which to lay her eggs. The caterpillar, which is yellowish, tinged with pink, pupates head downwards inside the hollowed stem where it has been feeding. The moth emerges in July and pushes its way out of a round " window " in the stem, already prepared by the caterpillar. The Sharks have narrow fore wings curved at the tip, which suggest a shark's fin cleaving the water, and most of them are named after their food-plants, such as the Mullein, Starwort, Cudweed, Wormwood, etc.

The Plusias are the only really beautiful *noctua*, and their names are descriptive : Beautiful Golden-Y, Plain Golden-Y, Gold Spot, Gold Spangle, Golden Plusia (which feeds on the leaves of Delphiniums), and the Burnished Brass, which eats Nettles. The Silver-Y is also a member of this group. The lovely Herald Moth, coloured in rust-red and grey, hibernates as a perfect insect, often in numbers, under the loose bark of dead or decaying trees.

The Old Lady (Plate **27** ; caterpillar—Plate **24**) is a large, drab, brown moth with frilly edges to its wings, and often comes into houses, attracted by the light. Two very large night-flying moths are the Goat Moth and the Leopard Moth. Their caterpillars bore their way right inside the trunks of trees, often killing them in the process, and take two or three years to reach their full size. The Goat Moth caterpillar is the colour of raw meat on the dorsal surface and paler underneath and has a very unpleasant smell.

Closely related to the Leopard moth are the Swifts, of which there are five species in Britain, the most familiar being the Ghost Swifts. The Swifts are a family of very primitive moths, whose rather long, narrow wings resemble in shape those of a dragonfly. They have long thin bodies and very short antennae. With the exception of the large Ghost Swift, whose male is white, their wings are a pale, dingy or golden brown, marked with whitish streaks and spots. They begin to fly at dusk and their caterpillars, which are a dirty white with brown heads, feed underground, on the roots of various plants such as nettle and dead nettle. The white males of the Ghost Swift may be seen swinging backwards and forwards just above the grass stems at dusk as though suspended by an invisible thread, but the much larger brown females fly in the normal manner. The Common Swift is smaller and can often be seen in large numbers at dusk darting over the pastures on an erratic course. It is usually plentiful in most districts during June. Others in the family are attractively named the Map-winged, Gold, and Orange Swifts. The caterpillar of the Northern Swift feeds on the roots of bracken. The larvae all feed underground on the roots of plants.

The Geometers

In this large group of Moths the caterpillars appear to measure their length as they move along. They are compelled to "loop", as they have no legs in the middle portion of their body, only the usual six thoracic legs and then two pairs of claspers on the hind segments. The majority feed after dusk and remain motionless, extended at an angle from the branch, like a stick or twig, during the daylight hours. This habit, combined with the usual way of moving, has given them the popular names of "stick caterpillars" or "loopers". The Moths usually have slender bodies and rather wide wings, but in some species, especially those which emerge during the winter, such as the Mottled Umber, Winter Moth and Pale Brindled Beauty, the females are wingless.

The Magpie Moth is known to all gardeners, as the caterpillars feed on Redcurrant and Goose-berry bushes, and the main colour scheme of black and white with yellow is carried through all stages of development. The family of Emerald

Moths are always admired for their lovely shades of green colouring, and the large, pale lemon-yellow Swallow-tail Moth looks more like a Butterfly than a Moth, with its curved and pointed hind wings. The caterpillars feed on green Privet and Ivy, and the Moth is quite often found in gardens during the height of summer.

The Thorns are a family of some dozen Moths, in shades of orange and yellow, looking rather like autumn leaves when found at rest during the day-time. Another group has the popular name of Beauty, but as they are mostly rather dull Moths, it is difficult to appreciate them. Included in this group is the Peppered Moth, which is particularly interesting, as it was the first species in which industrial melanism was recognized; now the black form has become the more common type.

There are a great number of Moths included in the family of Carpets, many of them beautifully marked to resemble lichens and mosses growing on the tree-trunks where they like to sit.

Among the smaller Moths is a group known as the Pugs, which includes over fifty species. Many of them are very similar, in shades of brown, but they can be identified as a family by the way in which they rest during the day, with their long narrow wings spread out flat against the surface on which they are resting, not folded over their bodies.

Moths have no set rules as to how they spend the winter; some species hibernate as living Moths, other pupate in autumn and emerge the following spring, while a certain number remain as caterpillars feeding on mild days, to complete their metamorphosis some time in the spring or early summer. To become an expert on Moths and their habits requires a lifetime's study, particularly if one includes the numerous tiny Moths of the Microlepidoptera.

Order COLEOPTERA. *Beetles*

Description. Minute to large insects, usually with hard bodies. The fore wings modified into horny elytra (wing-cases), hind wings membranous and folded below the elytra, or absent. Biting mouth-parts. Tarsi 5-jointed. Metamorphosis complete.

Classification. Two sub-orders. The ADEPHAGA, have usually filiform antennae. Both larvae and adults (imagines) are carnivorous. The POLYPHAGA have very varied antennae and tarsi. Feeding habits vary greatly. (Over 3,690 British species.)

Beetles are numerous everywhere, yet they are seldom seen. This is because they lead an unobtrusive life, being concealed from view, or nocturnal. Even the imagines are seldom seen by the admittedly notoriously unobservant non-naturalist, though we ourselves have nevertheless to search for them if we wish to see specimens. Everyone, however, knows the Ladybird Beetle, and perhaps the Tiger Beetle. These two exemplify the general aspect of Beetles as a whole. Although the order is exceedingly vast—over a quarter of a million species are already known to science—its members are somehow readily classed as Beetles by the non-expert, but the family Staphylinidae are perhaps rather puzzling when seen for the first time.

Beetles are essentially creatures of the soil itself. There they hunt other insects or Beetles. They live in refuse of all kinds, vegetable or animal, and in decaying organic matter. Many live in sound or in rotting wood, and yet other species feed on plants and trees and the fruits they bear. Every form of animal and vegetable product, dried or processed by man, has one or more coleopterous species that will feed upon it. Beetles of the genus *Anthrenus* attack the carefully dried treasures of museums, and they breed there, too, so that after a time many exhibits could be destroyed. Some Beetles even live by the sea and are regularly submerged by the tides.

The diversity of the food environment where the Beetle larvae develop means that every form of adaptation is to be met with. Essentially the range of anatomical difference between larvae is due to the manner in which food has to be obtained. If it has to be done by hunting, then the larva is active on its legs and has properly developed jaws for seizing prey. The larva of the Ladybird is of this type (Plate **35**, *9*), so is that of Ground Beetles (Plate **32**, *6*) and of the Great Diving Beetle, which lives in ponds (Plate **33**, *4*). When a larva develops surrounded by its food, such as the wood-feeders, then the jaws are adapted for their purpose and the legs are weak; in others the legs may be wanting and eyes may be entirely absent as well. The Carabid larva referred to above (Plate **32**, *6*), on the other hand, may have six simple eyes (*ocelli*), of great value to a hunter. When the larvae are full-grown they turn into pupae, usually with no protective covering, as in Butterflies and Moths, because the surroundings where pupation takes place afford all the safety needed. The time taken for larval development varies greatly, depending on the nutritional value of the food. Wood-feeders may take two or three years before reaching full growth.

Sub-order *ADEPHAGA*. *Carnivorous Beetles*
(Order COLEOPTERA)

This sub-order is noted for its predaceous carnivorous species, both terrestrial (*Carabidae*,

Tiger and Ground Beetles) and aquatic (*Dytiscidae*, Water Beetles and *Gyrinidae*, Whirligigs). The *Carabidae* comprise two sub-families, the *Cicindelinae* and *Carabinae*, which until fairly recently were classed as distinct families.

The larvae of the sub-order Adephaga are as predaceous as the adult insects. That of *Cicindela campestris*, the well-known Tiger Beetle, is, however, rather sluggish. It waits hidden in a vertical position in a hole in the ground, only the jaws projecting above the surface, and with these it seizes any small living prey that passes; the victims are devoured at the bottom of the hole. This Beetle (Plate **32**, *1*) frequents sandy places in spring and early summer. *C. sylvatica* (Plate **32**, *2*) is a close relation of more sombre colour. Among the family Carabinae the common *Carabus nemoralis* and *C. violaceus* (Plate **32**, *3, 4*) belong to the species described by Fabre as frenzied murderers. Carabid larvae (Plate **32**, *6*) are just as fierce. Not quite so closely related is *Brachinus crepitans* (Plate **32**, *5*), the Bombardier Beetle, so named because if chased it can squirt out an explosive liquid which volatizes immediately on reaching the air; this method of defence is possessed by several species. *Badister bipustulatus* (Plate **32**, *7*) is common in marshy places; it is slightly smaller than a similar species, *B. unipustulatus*, from which it differs particularly in the shape of the thorax.

The aquatic members of the sub-order Adephaga are as fierce as the terrestrial forms. The Great Diving Beetle, *Dytiscus marginalis* (Plate **33**, male—*5*, female—*3*), if kept in an aquarium will soon destroy every living creature in it. The male has on the front legs remarkable disc-like suckers used for grasping the female. Unlike most aquatic larvae, that of *Dytiscus* cannot breathe in water, and so has to go to the surface as the imagines are obliged to do. Air is taken in by projecting the hind quarters out of the water (Plate **33**, *4*). Quite the opposite obtains in the largest of all Water Beetles, *Hydrous* (=*Hydrophilus*) *piceus* (Plate **33**, *2*), which protrudes its head out of the water to obtain air. This is the Great Silver (or Diving) Water Beetle, named after the bubble of air which covers its underside as it swims down. The imago of this Beetle is vegetarian. It does not belong to the sub-order Adephaga, but is of the family Hydrophilidae of the sub-order Polyphaga. Its larva is, however, carnivorous.

Sub-order *POLYPHAGA*. *Omnivorous Beetles*
(Order COLEOPTERA)

The members of this sub-order are most diverse in anatomy and biology. They are also exceedingly numerous, the species being classified into families, superfamilies and larger groupings. A clear and useful idea of them can be obtained by setting out a simplified list as given opposite, and this also indicates the scientific families corresponding to popular names of the more common Beetles, some of which are referred to in this book.

We can allow ourselves here only a few general remarks on the Polyphaga, of which some family representatives are illustrated in colour on Plates **33** (*2*), **35**, **38** and **40**.

An important anatomical feature characteristic of Beetles is the pair of hard wing-cases, or elytra. In some species the elytra are, however, much reduced in length, exposing to view the abdominal segments. This is to be seen in the numerous Rove Beetles (family Staphylinidae), such as *Staphylinus caesareus* (Plate **35**, *1*), where the reduced elytra are well shown. This allows much flexibility of the abdomen. *Staphylinus olens*, the Devil's Coach-horse (Plate **35**, *5* ; and Plate **5**, *3*, showing difference between a Staphylinid and an Earwig) makes use of this to oppose danger by

POLYPHAGA

Larger Groupings	Families	Popular Names
STAPHYLINOIDEA	Staphylinidae	Rove Beetles.
	Silphidae	Burying and Carrion Beetles.
DIVERSICORNIA	Coccinellidae	Ladybird Beetles.
	Hydrophilidae	Land and Water Scavengers.
	Cantharidae	Soldier Beetles, Glow-worms, etc.
	Elateridae	Click Beetles.
HETEROMERA	Tenebrionidae	Nocturnal Ground Beetles.
	Meloïdae	Oil Beetles, Blister Beetles.
	Pyrochroidae	Cardinal Beetles.
PHYTOPHAGA	Chrysomelidae	Leaf Beetles.
	Cerambycidae	Longhorn Beetles.
RHYNCHOPHORA	Curculionidae	Weevils.
	Scolytidae	Bark Beetles.
LAMELLICORNIA	Lucanidae	Stag Beetles.
	Scarabaeidae	Chafers, Dung Beetles.

(*This list does not give a complete picture of the* COLEOPTERA, *but it is comprehensive in respect of our commoner species.*)

adopting a threatening attitude and emitting at the same time an unpleasant smell. The common *Creophilus maxillosus* (Plates **34** ; **35**, *2*) is another example from this family. The most interesting Oil Beetles (family Meloïdae) have similarly abbreviated elytra, as in *Meloë pro-scarabaeus* (Plate **38**, *6*). The well-known Glow-

85

worm is the female of *Lampyris noctiluca* (family Lampyridae, of the Diversicornia) in which all the abdominal segments are exposed (Plate **38**, *3*); the male (Plate **38**, *2*) has, however, complete elytra, as well as wings to take him to the female's " cold light ", which is a sexual call.

Cantharis abdominalis (Plate **38**, *4*) is a representative of the family Cantharidae, whose members have no photogenic (light-producing) organs as possessed by their cousins the Lampyridae. Other species, forming also part of the superfamily Diversicornia, are *Elater balteatus* (Plate **34**), often found in large numbers on Birch, though it is not common everywhere; *Cantharis rustica* (Plate **38**, *9*), which is common on flowers and shrubs; *Agriotes obscurus* (Plate **38**, *1*) is unfortunately all too common, its larvae being probably the commonest of our "wireworms". *Necrobia ruficollis* (Plate **34**) is another member; it is found in dry carcases and skins, and among bones. The species is celebrated among coleopterists because, in the words of Canon Fowler, it " saved the life of the celebrated Latreille : when imprisoned at Bordeaux during the French Revolution, he found a specimen of the insect on the walls of his cell, and sent it to M. Bory de St. Vincent, whom he knew to be interested in Entomology, and who had influence enough to secure his release ".

The superfamily Heteromera is named after the uneven number of joints in the tarsi of the insects comprising it, there being only four joints in the hind legs, the two other pairs having five joints. Included in it is *Pyrochroa coccinea* (Plate **38**, *7*), of the small family Pyrochroidae, the Cardinal Beetles, which may be found under the bark of decaying oak. The black head of the species distinguishes it immediately from *Pyrochroa serraticornis*, whose head is red; this Beetle is also smaller, and it is found on flowers and grasses.

Meloë proscarabaeus may be mentioned further as an example of " reflex-bleeding " (see page 15), another is *Timarcha tenebricosa* (Plate **38**, *8*), popularly called the Bloody-nosed Beetle because it pours out a red fluid (" blood ") from its mouth when it is touched or alarmed. The latter species, and *Chrysolina staphylaea* (Plate **38**, *10*), belong to the Chrysomelidae, a most extensive family of Leaf-eaters. Another member is the redoubtable *Leptinotarsa decemlineata* (Plate **31**), the Colorado Beetle, which came from America in 1875 and successfully established itself across the Channel. The Beetle is very destructive to growing potatoes. It has invaded England on several occasions, but so far it has been eliminated, thanks to immediate steps taken by the authorities ; when the Beetle is discovered it should be reported without delay to the police.

Rhagium bifasciatum (Plate **34**) is found in fir woods. Many Beetles of other families are to be found on leaves, though their larvae may feed on roots, etc. One of the most beautiful is *Cetonia aurata* (Plate **40**, *7*), the common Rose Chafer, as well as the familiar Cockchafer, *Melolontha melolontha* (or *vulgaris*) (Plate **40**, *8*), which is particularly " hairy " when freshly emerged (Plate **36**). These two species, included in the family Scarabaeidae, as well as members of the Curculionidae, the Weevils, such as *Hylobius abietis* (Plate **40**, *3*), are perhaps the best known to non-naturalists. Another familar Beetle, but restricted to southern England, is *Lucanus cervus* (Plate **37**, showing both male and female), the Stag Beetle ; only the male has the enlarged mandibles, which look like miniature stag antlers. This species varies much in size, and in size and shape of the " antlers ".

Other Beetles are destructive wood-borers, or live in decaying wood, as do the larvae of the Stag

Beetle (Plate **37**). Most of these insects belong to the family Cerambycidae, the Long-horns. They are attractively coloured, as *Aromia moschata* (Plate **40**, *2*), the Musk Beetle, *Saperda carcharias* (Plate **40**, *5*), *Strangalia maculata* (Plate **38**, *12*) and the active Wasp Beetle, *Clytus arietis* (Plate **40**, *1*), which mimics a wasp, particularly deceiving when visiting flowers in sunshine (Plate **36**).

Members of the family Scolytidae are Bark Beetles, though plants and fruits are also attacked by some species. These insects make the intricate tunnels often seen under the bark of many trees (Plate **39**, *1*); their life-histories are most interesting.

Some Beetles destroy or befoul man's stored food : such are *Tenebrio molitor* (Plate **38**, *5*), of the family Tenebrionidae, whose larvae are known to bakers as Meal Worms, and another is *Blaps mucronata* (Plate **38**, *11*), which has a particularly unpleasant smell. Its larvae eat decaying vegetable matter in cellars, bakeries and other dark retreats.

A number of species among the sub-order Polyphaga are carnivorous, the best-known being the Ladybird Beetles (family Coccinellidae), of which there are several species. They often vary much in markings, except *Coccinella septempunctata* (Plate **35**, *6* ; pupa and larva—*8*, *9*), the Seven-spot Ladybird. Both the larvae and the adults feed voraciously on small insects, especially Aphids. *Anatis ocellata* (Plate **35**, *7*), the Eyed Ladybird, is our largest species ; it is found on Firs.

Some Beetles, such as the family Silphidae, are useful scavengers of dead animals and birds, both they and their larvae feeding on them. *Necrophorus investigator*, *N. humator* and *N. vespillo* (Plate **35**, *3*) are examples of Beetles which actually bury, say a bird, by digging the ground away from

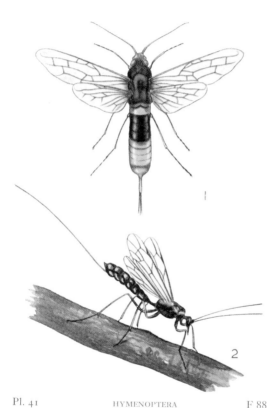

1. Greater Horntail, *Uroceras gigas*, female. 2. Its parasite, *Rhyssa persuasoria*, female, the largest British Ichneumon. (*Both natural size.*) *Pages* 92, 96.

Pl. 42   HYMENOPTERA (SYMPHYTA) : SAWFLIES
Left : Abia sericea *ovipositing in a leaf.*   *Right :* Larvae on Birch.
(Both approx. natural size.) Page 93.

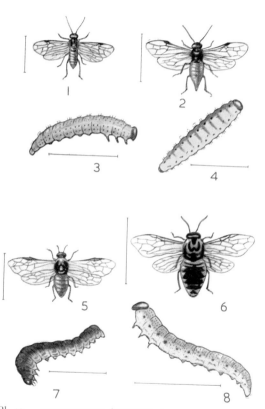

Pl. 43   HYMENOPTERA (SYMPHYTA): SAWFLIES

Gooseberry Sawfly, *Nematus ribesii*—1. Female;
3. Larva. Poplar Sawfly, *Trichiocampus viminalis*—2.
Female; 4. Larva. Turnip Sawfly, *Athalia rosae*
—5. Female; 7. Larva. Pine Sawfly, *Diprion pini*—
6. Female; 8. Larva. *Page* 93.

Pl. 44   HYMENOPTERA

Above : Sawfly larva showing characteristic curled-up attitude (× 3), *pages* 92, 93. *Below :* The cells of Leaf-cutter Bees (family Megachilidae) are made from circles of leaf cut from Rose bushes, etc., as well as from petals (*half natural size*), *p.* 100.

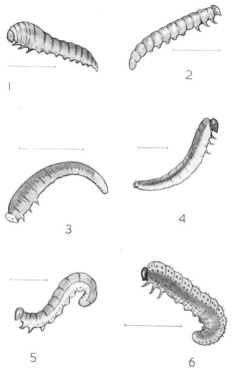

Pl. 45   HYMENOPTERA (SYMPHYTA): SAWFLY
LARVAE

1. A Slugworm, *Caliroa cerasi*. 2. Apple Sawfly
Hoplocampa testudinea. 3. A Rose-leaf Sawfly,
Allantus cinctus. 4. Another Rose-leaf Sawfly, *Blen-nocampa pusilla*. 5. Palisade Sawfly, *Stauronematus compressicornis*. 6. Another Rose-feeder, *Arge ochropus*
(=*rosae*). Pages 92, 94.

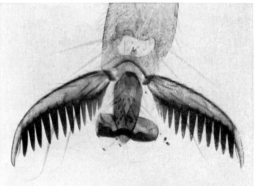

Pl. 46   HYMENOPTERA (PARASITICA)

Above : Ovipositor or Egg-placer of Yellow Ophion.
Below : Claw of Ichneumon used when seizing hold of
its victim when the egg is being laid. (*Both greatly
enlarged.*) *Page* 96.

Pl. 47   HYMENOPTERA (PARASITICA)

Above : Grubs of an Ichneumon (family Braconidae) crawling out of a Large White caterpillar. *Below :* Two minutes later—there is no trace of the larvae, whose cocoons were spun without delay. The host caterpillar now dies and will shrivel up. (*Both natural size.*) *Page* 97.

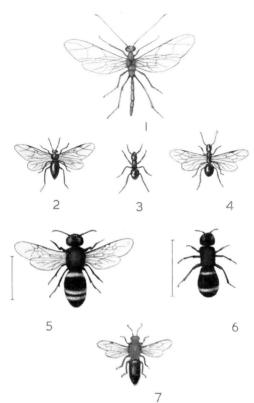

Pl. 48   HYMENOPTERA (ACULEATA)

1. Common Yellow Ophion, *Ophion luteus*, *p.* 96.
Wood Ant, *Formica rufa*—2. Male; 3. Worker;
4. Female; *page* 98. Velvet Ant, *Mutilla europaea*—
5. Male; 6. Female; *page* 99. 7. A Ruby-tail, *Chrysis
ignita*, *p.* 99. (*All natural size, except* 5 *and* 6.)

Pl. 49   PLANT GALLS CAUSED BY HYMENOPTERA

Above : Pupa of the Marble Gall Wasp, *Adleria kollari* (× 7), *p.* 97. The hard galls caused by this species are common on Oak, especially on young trees.
Below : Fully developed pupa of the Oak Apple Gall Wasp, *Biorrhiza terminalis* (× 5), *p.* 97. This gall is fleshy and moist.

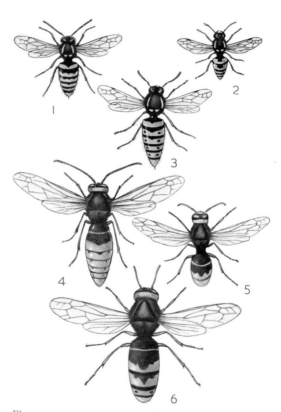

Pl. 50   HYMENOPTERA (ACULEATA)

Common Wasp, *Vespula* (= *Vespa*) *vulgaris*—1. Male;
2. Worker;   3. Female;   *p*. 98.   Hornet, *Vespa
crabro*—4. Male;   5. Worker;   6. Female;   *p*. 98.

Above : Gooden's Homeless Bee, *Nomada goodeniana*
($\times 3\frac{1}{2}$), *p.* 99. *Below :* Female Hornet, *Vespa
crabro* ($\times 1\frac{1}{2}$), *p.* 98.

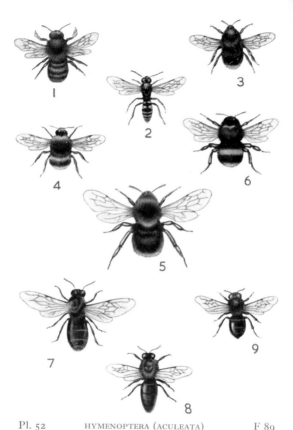

1 *Megachile maritima*, male. 2. *Nomada marshamella*, male. 3. *Bombus lapidarius*, worker. 4. *B. pratorum*, worker. 5. A Cuckoo Bee, *Psithyrus campestris*, female. 6. *Bombus terrestris*, worker. Hive or Honey Bee, *Apis mellifera*—7. Male; 8. Female; 9. Worker. (*All natural size.*) *Pages* 98–99.

underneath the animal, and there the female will lay her eggs, usually in pairs. Besides these useful species, known as Burying Beetles, there are many Carrion Beetles which do not act as sextons, but whose larvae and imagines help in clearing away carcases. *Oeceoptoma thoracicum* (Plate **35**, *4*) will often be found near carrion, to which it is attracted by the smell of decay, as are all these Beetles. A close-up of this insect's head and thorax is also given (Plate **31**). Other Beetles with unpleasant but useful feeding habits belong to the Scarabaeidae, a family celebrated by Fabre. In addition to the root and decaying leaf-eaters of this family, already mentioned, there are those who feed on dung (usually that of herbivorous animals). *Geotrupes stercorarius* (Plate **40**, *4*), sometimes called the Dor Beetle, is of these, so is *Typhaeus typhaeus* (Plate **40**, *6*; male; the two thorn-like projections at the front of the thorax are absent in the female).

Order STREPSIPTERA. *Stylops*

Description. Minute insects, usually parasites of other insects. Males winged. Branched antennae. Mouth-parts degenerate, originally biting type. Fore wings reduced to halteres or balancers, hind wings large. Females degenerate, wingless, usually legless, and have the appearance of larvae.

Classification. There are four British families. The order is closely related to the COLEOPTERA, Beetles. (16 British species.)

The larval stages are passed as internal parasites of certain wasps, such as those of the genera *Vespa*, *Vespula*, and bees, especially *Halictus* and *Andrena*. The female Stylops passes the whole of her life in the host, from whose sides the parasite may be seen protruding between the

Bee's segments. The Stylops absorbs body-fluids of the host without destroying vital organs, but the genitalia are adversely affected. "Stylopized" hosts may often be recognized by their misshapen abdomen. The males are completely formed winged insects, having very elaborate antennae. Pairing takes place on the host. For illustrations and details of these very interesting insects see " Beetles of the British Isles ", one of the Wayside and Woodland Series of books published by Frederick Warne and Co. Ltd.

Order HYMENOPTERA. *Sawflies, Ants, Bees,
Wasps, Ichneumons, Gall Wasps*

Description. Four membranous wings, the hind smaller than the fore wings and having interlocking hooklets allowing fore and hind wings to act as one. Mouth-parts adapted for biting, lapping or sucking. Ovipositor always present but may be functionally modified for sawing or stinging. Metamorphosis complete.

Classification. Two sub-orders, SYMPHYTA, having no marked constriction or waist between the abdomen and thorax, and thus also referred to as *SESSILIVENTRES*—trochanters 2-jointed, larvae generally possessing thoracic and abdominal legs ; and APOCRITA with the waist generally very evident, hence also referred to as *PETIOLATA*—trochanters 1- or 2-jointed, larvae legless.

The Apocrita are for convenience divided into ACULEATA, the stinging forms, and the PARASITICA, which parasitize other insects. (Over 6,191 British species.)

Hymenoptera is the order to which the least justice can be done in any popular book on insects.

This is due not only to the exceedingly vast number of species, but especially also to their highly evolved life-histories. The different species have habits that are most complex, and at the same time often differ very much from each other. Thus any descriptions chosen can only illustrate isolated examples of the wonders to be observed in other species.

All hymenopterous species undergo the complete cycle of insect metamorphosis, egg, larva, pupa and imago all being present. An important feature is that the majority of their larvae must be provided by the parents with food, as they are unable to seek it themselves. Thus in what are known as the " solitary " species the female has to make all arrangements for concealing her egg (or eggs) and providing food adjacent to it for the larva when it emerges. Some of these solitary species live in colonies, but each individual works independently for its progeny. Evolution has progressed further in what are known as the " social " species, as instanced by Ants and many Bees and Wasps, whose division of labour for the provision of food for future generations becomes highly complex. The advanced degree of social behaviour attained in Hymenoptera is equalled only by one other order, the Isoptera (Termites), but these insects do not occur in the British Isles.

An anatomical feature of great importance in connection with the behaviour of many of these insects is the ovipositor (egg-placer). It is used for penetrating matter in which the female wishes to lay her eggs. In some species the ovipositor is modified for sawing, boring, piercing or stinging. The stinging apparatus consists of two poison glands (page 14), these being highly specialized.

Sub-order *SYMPHYTA.* *Sawflies, and Horntails or Woodwasps*
(Order HYMENOPTERA)

This sub-order is sometimes called *PHYTO-
PHAGA*, Plant-eaters, or *SESSILIVENTRES*, because
the abdomen is broadly sessile with the thorax
(i.e., there is no constriction between these two
parts of the body). Its members are less
specialized than those of the second sub-order
(*APOCRITA*), but the ovipositor is modified for
sawing or boring. The larvae also differ in that
they fend for themselves, being provided with
true (thoracic) legs as well as six or more pairs
of abdominal prolegs, the latter of course being
present only during larval life as in the case of
caterpillars of Butterflies and Moths (LEPI-
DOPTERA).

The *SYMPHYTA* are divided into two super-
families, the *Tenthredinoidea* and the *Oryssoidea*.
The latter need not concern us here, except to
mention that parasitism, general as it is in
hymenopterous insects, is known in SYMPHYTA
only in species of the genus *Oryssus*: there is
only one rare British species.

(*Typical SYMPHYTA are illustrated in colour on
Plates* **41**, *1*, **43**, *and* **45**).

The Uroceridae (Siricidae), known as Horntails or
Woodwasps, is a family of large brilliantly coloured
insects whose larvae are wood-borers of trees.
Urocerus gigas, the Greater Horntail (Plate **41**,
1) of fir woods, is the largest species we have.
It is typical of its kind in appearance and colouring,
though several species are metallic-blue. It is
often mistaken for the Hornet (Plate **48**) because
of its sting-like projection, which is the ovipositor
of the female, and the black-and-yellow arrangement of its colours. The ovipositor of the Horn-

tail is used for boring into bark to deposit an egg in the wood. The larva bores into the heart of the tree, and can do considerable damage ; there are several records of Horntails emerging from wood that was covered by sheet metal.

In Sawflies, the ovipositor is modified into saws, enabling these insects literally to saw leaves and make incisions in plant stems. *Abia sericea* is shown on a leaf in Plate **42**. The Stem Sawflies (Cephidae) are a family of small insects whose larvae bore in the stems and shoots of plants to feed upon the pith. The larger Sawflies belong to other families, the majority to Tenthredinidae.

Leaf-eating Sawfly larvae bear much resemblance to the caterpillars of Butterflies and Moths. They may be distinguished from them in that the Sawfly larvae have (in addition to three pairs of thoracic legs) six or more pairs of abdominal legs (prolegs), whereas in Butterflies and Moths there are never more than five pairs. When fully grown the larvae make cocoons on the food-plants or, less frequently, in the soil. Sawflies are best known in their larval state, and this is especially so in those found on roses and fruit-bushes. Like caterpillars, they are of various colours, and they have a peculiar habit of curling the posterior segments of the body away from the leaf on which they are feeding (Plate **42**). The following larvae are well known.

Nematus ribesii (Plate **43**, *3*), larva of the Gooseberry Sawfly, Plate **43**, *1*, female. Also found on currants.

Trichiocampus viminalis (Plate **43**, *4*), larva of the Poplar Sawfly, Plate **43**, *2*, female.

Athalia rosae (Plate **43**, *7*), larva of the Turnip Sawfly, Plate **43**, *5*, female.

Diprion pini (Plate **43**, *8*), larva of the Pine Sawfly, Plate **43**, *6*, female.

Caliroa cerasi (Plate **45**, *1*) feeds on Oak, Birch and Willow, being one of the larvae popularly referred to as Slugworms, which are also found on roses.

Hoplocampa testudinea (Plate **45**, *2*), larva of the Apple Sawfly ; it feeds on the newly-formed fruit.

Allantus cinctus (Plate **45**, *3*) is a Rose-leaf feeder.

Blennocampa pusilla (Plate **45**, *4*) also feeds on Rose leaves, concealing itself whilst doing so by turning the edge of the leaf over itself.

Stauronematus compressicornis (Plate **45**, *5*) feeds on Poplar, and is the famous Palisade Sawfly larva, so called because it forms with saliva a series of little posts round the area on the leaf on which it is feeding.

Arge ochropus (=*rosae*) (Plate **45**, *6*). Common on Roses, southern half of England.

Sub-order *APOCRITA*. *Ants, Bees, Wasps, Ichneumons, Gall Wasps.* (Order HYMENOPTERA)

All members of this sub-order have a well-defined (petiolate) waist, hence these insects are also called *PETIOLATA*. They have also been called *HETEROPHAGA*, suggesting their varied diet. There are numerous species of *APOCRITA*, all having extremely varied and interesting life-histories. The adults are usually highly specialized in their habits, which in some species has resulted in the forming of social communities. Most HYMENOPTERA belong to the present sub-order which may be divided further into *PARASITICA*, comprising insects of specialized parasitical habits, and *ACULEATA*, species having stings. The literature on the

Parasitica and Aculeata is vast and the amount added to it every year reflects the importance of many of these insects' activities to man's economy. Many Parasitica, for example, have furnished allies to combat pestiferous insects; nearly all of the latter belong to other orders.

The diversity of habits may be gathered from the popular names given to some of these insect families, as given here :—

APOCRITA

Larger groupings and superfamilies	Families	Popular names
PARASITICA (Parasitical species).		
ICHNEUMONOIDEA	*Ichneumonidae*	Ichneumon-wasps.
	Braconidae	,,
CHALCIDOIDEA	*Chalcididae*	Chalcids.
CYNIPOIDEA	*Cynipidae*	Gall Wasps.
ACULEATA (Stinging species)		
FORMICOIDEA, Ants	*Formicidae*	Ants.
	Mutillidae	Velvet Ants.
	Chrysididae	Cuckoo-wasps, Ruby-tails.
VESPOIDEA, Wasps	*Vespidae*	Wasps.
	Eumenidae	Solitary Wasps, Potter and Mason Wasps.
	Pompilidae	Spider Wasps.
SPHECOIDEA, Wasps	*Sphecidae*	Digger Wasps.
	Andrenidae	Mining Bees.
	Megachilidae	Leaf-cutter Bees.
	Nomadidae	Homeless Bees.
APOIDEA, Bees	*Anthrophoridae*	Potter Flower Bees.
	Bombidae	Bumble or Humble Bees.
	Apidae	Hive Bees.

(*Typical species of* APOCRITA *are shown in colour on Plates* 41, 2, 48, 50, 52, 53.)

PARASITICA. The most important parasites which limit the unchecked multiplication of the insect legions belong to the extensive super-families of Ichneumonoidea (Ichneumon-wasps) and Chalcidoidea (Chalcids). The latter are less known, but they are of even greater importance than the Ichneumons.

Ichneumons are slender insects with long antennae, which are constantly in motion. The antennae—and, of course, the four wings of all members of the order Hymenoptera—readily distinguish them from True Flies (order Diptera). The appearance of our largest species, *Rhyssa persuasoria* (Plate **41**, *2*) is typical of an Ichneumon, the long ovipositor showing that this one is a female. In some mysterious way this insect is able to detect where the larva of the Greater Horn-tail (Plate **41**, *1*, shows the female imago) lies concealed within the tree. It then proceeds to bore into the wood with its flimsy-looking ovipositor in order to lay an egg on or near the larva. On emergence the Ichneumon larva will feed on that of the Sawfly, which it will destroy. The Horntail and its parasite are confined to pine-woods, and are therefore not seen as frequently as the Common Yellow Ophion, *Ophion luteus* (Plate **48**, *1*), an Ichneumon which parasitizes caterpillars of several of our larger moths, such as that of the Puss Moth. Plate **46** shows the ovipositor of the Yellow Ophion, and the claw used to hold the victim while the egg is laid.

Parasitism of every conceivable form exists, and insects in all stages of development are subject to attack. The relationship between species of the group Parasitica and their hosts is often very specifically restricted (e.g., between *Rhyssa persuasoria* and the Greater Horntail), and this has permitted many spectacular successes of applied entomology to be achieved under the heading of Biological Control. An incident of this is shown in Plate 47.

The family Cynipidae includes many species which are parasites of plants and trees. Some of these small insects are gall-causers on leaves, flowers, stems and roots; others do not cause galls, but live as lodgers, taking up residence with a gall-causer, with whom they then live in close proximity without doing any harm to the rightful owner. These lodgers may be other Cynipids, or larvae of Lepidoptera, Coleoptera or Diptera. There are yet other species which are true parasites of other Cynipidae.

The galls are caused by the living larva (Plate 49) after emergence from the egg, the presence of which modifies the form taken by the growing plant tissues. A remarkable feature of galls is that the form and colour of a gall on a particular plant or tree will be characteristic of a definite species of insect. Galls are in fact as varied as the insects themselves. It appears, however, that insects of the same genus produce galls of a similar type even on plants that are not closely related. Not all galls are due to insects, however.

ACULEATA. The ovipositor of these insects is modified into a sting, and can no longer be used for laying eggs. The eggs are laid from an opening at the base of the ovipositor. In Ants the sting is present only in the females and workers in the case of a number of carnivorous species. In other Ants the sting is vestigial or absent, and these species are considered to be more evolved; furthermore, they have become vegetarian—as are most British species.

All Ants belong to the family Formicidae. Ants pair in a nuptial or marriage flight; the female on descending to earth rids herself of her wings and seeks a suitable site wherein to prepare a brood chamber. She will never leave this chamber, where she lays her first eggs. When the larvae appear they are fed with secretions from her salivary glands. After a while the larvae pupate, and eventually adult Ants emerge. These are workers who henceforth relieve their mother of all cares. They make a passage from the brood chamber to the outside world, where they forage for food. The mother or queen now attends to nothing else but egg-laying; she is fed by the workers. Some females have been known to live like this for fifteen years. In midsummer males and females appear which at a chosen moment fly away on their marriage flight. One of our most familiar species is the Wood Ant, *Formica rufa* (Plate **48**, *2*—male, *4*—female, both shown with wings " set " ; *3*—worker, which never has wings). Ants form permanent communities of numerous individuals. The Wood Ant nest, for example, may have a population of as many as 100,000 individuals ; in another species 500,000 Ants were found in one formicary. Volumes have been written on the life-histories of Ants, on the other creatures that live with them as guests, on their flocks of Aphids, on the parasites of other insect orders which live in the nests and destroy Ant larvae, and so on.

Other social insects are the Wasps (family Vespidae), such as *Vespula* (= *Vespa*) *vulgaris*, the Common Wasp (Plate **50**, *1*—male or drone, *2*—worker, *3*—female or queen) ; our only Hornet, *Vespa crabro* (Plate **50**, *4*—male, *5*—worker, *6*—female, also Plate **51**), as well as the Bumble Bees (family Bombidae) whose workers are well known, such as *Bombus lapidarius* (Plate **52**, *3*), *B. pratorum* (Plate **52**, *4*), *B. terrestris* (Plate **52**, *6*). *Apis mellifera* (Plate **52**, *7*—male, *8*—female, *9*—worker) is the common Hive Bee. There is considerable variation in the habits and life-histories of different species of social insects. The underground nest of a common social insect, the Wasp *Vespula germanica*, is shown on Plate **39**, *2*.

Social species have close relatives who are parasites on them. *Psithyrus campestris* (Plate **52**, *5*—female) is a Cuckoo Bee parasite of *Bombus*; after killing the *Bombus* queen she lays her own eggs, the *Psithyrus* larvae being cared for by the *Bombus* workers. Of the Velvet Ants (family Mutillidae, which are not Ants, however) *Mutilla europaea* (Plate **48**, *5*—male, *6*—female, wingless in all species) also parasitizes *Bombus*. The larvae of *Chrysis ignita* (Plate **48**, *7*), one of the Ruby-tails (family Chrysididae), feeds upon other members of the order Hymenoptera.

Other species lead blameless lives. *Eumenes coarctata* (Plate **53**, *3*) is a Potter Wasp (family Vespidae, formerly included in a separate family, the Eumenidae), named after its small pot-shaped nest. Spider Wasps (Pompilidae, an extensive family) paralyze spiders by stinging them ; they do not kill them. *Anoplius fuscus* (Plate **53**, *1*) buries such victims in an excavated hole, an egg being laid on each spider so that the larva on emergence will have a provision of preserved food. Such insects are solitary species, as are the families of Sphecidae Wasps (Plate **53**, *2*, *4*, *5*, and *7* being examples), and of *Prosopis* Bees (Plate **53**, *8*, *Prosopis signata*). Another genus, Andrena (Plate **53**, *6*, *Andrena armata*), also comprises solitary species, though the females of these tend to congregate in colonies. They are parasitized by species of the genus *Nomada*, such as Gooden's Homeless Bee, *Nomada goodeniana* (Plate **51**), and *Nomada marshamella* (Plate **52**, *2*, male). *Megachile maritima* (Plate **52**,

99

1, male), belongs to the Leaf-cutters (genus *Megachile*—see Plate **44**). The work of these species is well known from the neat circles they cut out of leaves. The family also includes parasitic and other species.

Order DIPTERA. *True Flies*

Description. Two membranous wings, the hind pair modified into halteres or balancers. Mouth-parts adapted for sucking, sometimes for piercing. Segments of thorax fused. Metamorphosis complete.

Classification. There are three sub-orders, this being particularly evinced by the larval and pupal stages : the NEMATOCERA, larvae well developed, head free or exserted, horizontally biting mandibles, antennae of imago (adult) longer than head and thorax and many jointed ; BRACHYCERA, larvae with incompletely developed head which can be withdrawn within the body, antennae of imago shorter than thorax, very variable and having usually 3 joints, the last elongate ; the CYCLORRHAPHA, head of the larva is vestigial, antennae of imago 3-jointed. (Over 5,200 British species.)

An entomologist does not use the word " fly " indiscriminately, for to him it refers only to the two-winged insects of the Diptera. The order is extensive, comprising insects which are mainly active in daylight, especially in sunshine. They visit flowers for nectar, or decaying animal or plant refuse ; others are predatory on insects, whilst the females of many species are bloodsuckers of animals and birds. The feeding habits make many of them dangerous carriers or transmitters of disease. The vectors of malaria, yellow fever and sleeping sickness are species of Diptera. The following tabulation gives the popular names

of a selection of Flies, and shows how the families
are arranged in the classification of the order.

DIPTERA

Sub-order *NEMATOCERA*
    Tipulidae — Crane-flies or Daddy-long-legs.
    Culicidae — Mosquitoes, Gnats.
    Chironomidae — Midges.
    Cecidomyiidae — Gall Midges.
    Mycetophilidae — Fungus Gnats.

Sub-order *BRACHYCERA*
    Stratiomyidae — Soldier Flies.
    Tabanidae — Clegs, Horse Flies, Gadflies.
    Asilidae — Robber Flies.
    Bombyliidae — Bee Flies.

Sub-order *CYCLORRHAPHA*
    Syrphidae — Hover Flies.
    Conopidae — Thick-headed Flies.
    Larvaevoridae (*Tachinidae*) — Parasitic Flies.
    Calliphoridae — Blue Bottles, Green Bottles, Blow Flies.
    Oestridae — Warble or Bot Flies.
    Muscidae — House Flies, Stable Flies.
    Hippoboscidae — Forest Flies, Sheep Keds.
    Nycteribiidae — Bat Lice.
    Braulidae — Bee Lice.

The Larvae of Diptera. The habits of
larvae often excite more curiosity than do the
other stages of an insect's life-history, even when
it is a species in which complete metamorphosis
exists. Flies have a greater diversity of larval
habits than is to be observed in any other order,
and we have seen how the structure of larvae
differs according to the sub-order. Some of them
are plant feeders, often being very destructive
pests, others are useful scavengers, feeding on

rotting animal and vegetable matter. Many larvae are useful parasites, checking the increase of other insects, though among these larvae are also harmful parasites of mammals, including man. The specialized morphological adaptation to their surroundings may be seen from examination of the larva of a Crane-fly which feeds on roots. It is the gardener's Leatherjacket, having a hard skin and a distinct head, provided with biting mouth-parts and antennae. The larva of our largest Crane-fly, *Tipula maxima* (Plate **55**, *1*— imago; Plate **54**, *1*—larva), lives in wet banks of ponds and streams; the lobes at the posterior end are for breathing. The anal breathing gills are more developed and conspicuous in the aquatic "Blood-worm", which is the larva of *Chironomus* (Plate **54**, *4*), also having pseudopods (false legs), close to the small head as well as on the last abdominal segment.

The larvae of the family Ptychopteridae live in shallow water in mud and debris, breathing being assured by a long "tail", held upwards (Pl. **54**, *2*). A similar projection to enable easy respiration may be seen in a Syrphid larva, the Rat-tailed Maggot (Plate **54**, *6*). The *Stratiomys* larva (Plate **54**, *3*) has a row of hairs to buoy it up at the surface of the water so as to leave the anal spiracles (breathing holes) exposed to the air.

A Mosquito larva ("Wriggler") (Plate **54**, *9*— *Culex*, *10*—*Anopheles*) breathes through a tube which has to be protruded periodically above the surface of the water (Plate **54**, *11*, *Culex*—A, *Anopheles*—B). It will suffocate if it cannot do this. Mosquito control is effected by applying a coat of oil over the surface of the water. This clogs up the tubes, and the smallest amount of oil is sufficient. *Culex pipiens* is the annoying blood-sucker known to everyone. *Anopheles maculipennis* is a carrier of malaria. Certain characteristic differences between the two kinds of Mosquitoes (of which there are many species) are shown in the illustrations already referred to on Plate **54**.

Breathing appendages ("tails", "pad-like" gills, etc.) are as usual absent from larvae which live surrounded by fresh air, such as that of another Syrphid (Plate **54**, 5) of the kind which prey on Aphids. They breathe in the normal adult way, through spiracles.

Sub-order *NEMATOCERA*
(Order DIPTERA)

This sub-order includes the most primitive Flies. Besides the Crane-flies or Daddy-long-legs (family Tipulidae, Plate **55**, *1, Tipula maxima*), whose larvae are especially destructive to roots, there are species which are of great medical importance because of their being disease-transmitting Mosquitoes of the family Culicidae. Midge-bites are due to members of the family Cerato-pogonidae. In the family Cecidomyiidae, the Gall Midges, are many species of economic interest due to their destructive attacks on cereals. Many of the Gnats whose larvae feed on fungi are members of the family Mycetophilidae.

Sub-order *BRACHYCERA*
(Order DIPTERA)

The females of Horse Flies and Clegs (family Tabanidae) are noisy insects which are blood-suckers of cattle, inflicting painful bites. *Tabanus bromius* (Plate **55**, 5), a Gad-fly, is common during the warmer months of the year. Male Tabanids visit flowers. The Asilidae, Robber Flies, form the largest family of the sub-order. They are hunters of other insects which they catch on the wing. The illustrations of the large *Asilus* *crabroniformis* (Plate **55**, *4*—female) and the very common *Dioctria rufipes* (Plate **55**, *2*—female) show their characteristically powerful legs. The family *Bombyliidae*, Bee Flies, as instanced by *Bombylius major* (Plate **55**, *3*), resemble Bumble Bees in appearance ; the larvae of many species of this family are parasites of Bees, such as *Andrena* and *Halictus*.

Sub-order CYCLORRHAPHA
(Order DIPTERA)

Among the Hover Flies (family Syrphidae) is another mimic of Bumble Bees. It is *Volucella bombylans* (Plate **57**, *3*—female), a species which varies much in colouring, and the larvae of which are found in the nests of Bees. They have also been found in those of the Wasp *Vespula* (= *Vespa*) *germanica*, to which of course the imago bears no resemblance. The more familiar colouring of a Hover Fly is to be seen in the common *Helophilus pendulus* (Plate **57**, *1*—female). Members of the family Conopidae are internal parasites of adult Wasps and Bees, *Physocephala rufipes* (Plate **57**, *2*) resembles a Sand Wasp (*Ammophila*, of the family Sphecidae).

One of the housewife's pet aversions is the Blue Bottle, also referred to as the Blow Fly. The Green Bottle is just as unpopular. The insects (all belonging to the family Calliphoridae) enter the kitchen to lay eggs on meat, etc., for their larvae are scavengers. *Calliphora vomitoria* (Plate **57**, *5*—female) is the common Blue Bottle. *Lucilia caesar* (Plate **57**, *4*) is the common Green Bottle, which seldom enters houses. Numbers of *Pollenia rudis* (Plate **60**, *1*), the Cluster Fly, occasionally enter attics. They keep closely together in clusters when at rest indoors, hence their name. Included in the family Muscidae we have the Common House Fly, *Musca domestica* (Plate **58**, *1*),

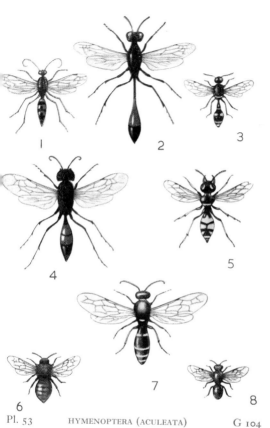

Pl. 53   HYMENOPTERA (ACULEATA)   G 104

1. A Spider Wasp, *Anoplius fuscus*. 2. *Ammophila sabulosa*. 3. A Potter Wasp, *Eumenes coarctata*. 4. *Podalonia hirsuta*. 5. *Crabro cribrarius*. 6. *Andrena armata*. 7. *Gorytes mystaceus*. 8. *Prosopis signata*. (*All females, slightly enlarged.*)   Page 99.

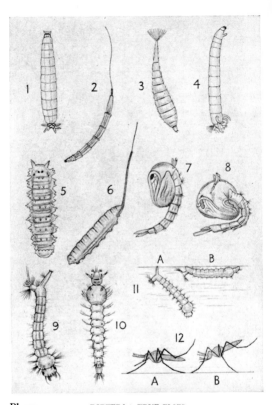

Pl. 54   DIPTERA : TRUE FLIES

Larvae : 1. Leatherjacket, *Tipula maxima*. 2. *Ptychoptera*. 3. *Stratiomys*. 4. Blood-worm, *Chironomus*. 5. Predatory Syrphid. 6. Rat-tailed Maggot. *Pages 102, 103.* Comparison of *Culex* and *Anopheles* (malaria-carrier) Mosquitoes—7 to 12, *pages 102–103.*

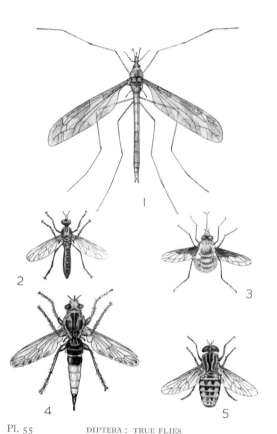

Pl. 55   DIPTERA : TRUE FLIES

1. Crane-fly, *Tipula maxima*. 2. A Robber Fly,
Dioctria rufipes. 3. Bee Fly, *Bombylius major*. 4. A
Robber Fly, *Asilus crabroniformis*, female. 5. Gad-fly,
Tabanus bromius. (*All natural size.*) *Pages* 103–104.

Pl. 56   DIPTERA: PARASITIC FLIES

Family Larvaevoridae. *Above :* Adult just emerged
from the cocoon of a Moth. The Fly's wings are not
yet developed ($\times$ 2). *Below :* Adult with wings fully
developed (*approx.* $\times$ 3¼). *Page* 105.

Pl. 57 DIPTERA : TRUE FLIES

1. A Hover Fly, *Helophilus pendulus*, female. 2. A
Thick-headed Fly, *Physocephala rufipes*. 3. A Hover
Fly, *Volucella bombylans*. 4. A Green Bottle, *Lucilia
caesar*. 5. Blue Bottle, *Calliphora vomitoria*, female.
(*All* × 1½, *except* 2—× 1¾.) Page 104.

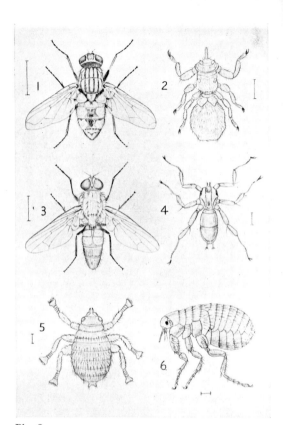

Pl. 58   DIPTERA, APHANIPTERA

DIPTERA: 1. House Fly, *Musca domestica*.   2. Sheep
Ked, *Melophagus ovinus*.   3. Lesser House Fly, *Fannia
canicularis*.   4. Bat Louse, *Nycteribia biarticulata*.   5.
Bee Louse, *Braula coeca*. *Pages* 104–106. APHANIPTERA:
6. Human Flea, *Pulex irritans*, *p.* 107.

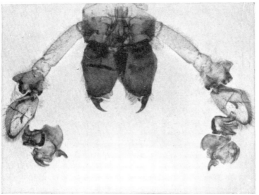

Pl. 59   ARANEAE : SPIDERS

Above : A Hunting Spider, *Pisaura listeri,* showing the chelicerae or fangs. *Below :* Chelicerae or fangs and complex palpi of a male Spider. (*Both greatly enlarged.*) Page 110.

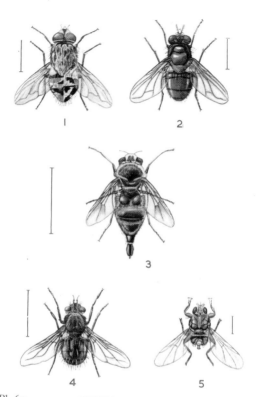

Pl. 60   DIPTERA : TRUE FLIES

1. Cluster Fly, *Pollenia rudis*. 2. A Green Bottle, *Orthellia cornicina*, female. 3. A Horse Bot Fly, *Gasterophilus intestinalis*, female. 4. A Parasitic Fly, *Larvaevora fera*, female. 5. A Bird parasite, *Ornithomya avicularia*, female. *Pages* 104–105.

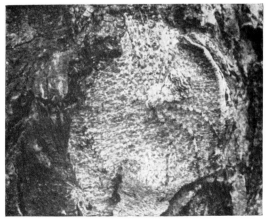

Pl. 61   ARANEAE : SPIDERS

Above : An active, sun-loving Hunting Spider, *Pisaura listeri* (13 *mm.*, ½ *in.*), *p.* 112.   *Below :* A Crab Spider of the genus *Philodromus*, *p.* 114.

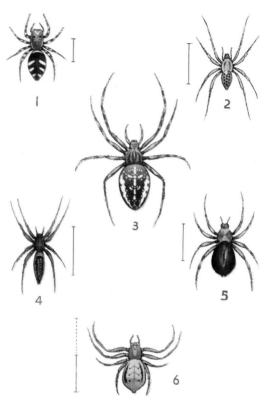

Pl. 62   ARANEAE : SPIDERS

1. Zebra Spider, *Salticus scenicus*. 2. A House Spider, *Tegenaria domestica*. 3. Garden Spider, *Aranea diadema*. 4. A Hunting Spider, *Pisaura listeri*. 5. Water Spider, *Argyroneta aquatica*. 6. A Crab Spider, *Misumena calycina*. Pages 111–114.

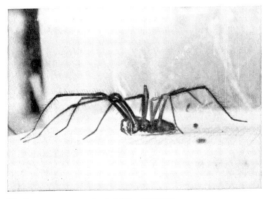

Pl. 63   ARANEAE : SPIDERS

Above : Micrommata viridissima, a fast-moving, brilliantly coloured Spider, male (*length of body—* 13 mm., ½ in.), p. 114. *Below :* A House Spider, *Tegenaria atrica* (19 mm., ¾ in.), p. 114.

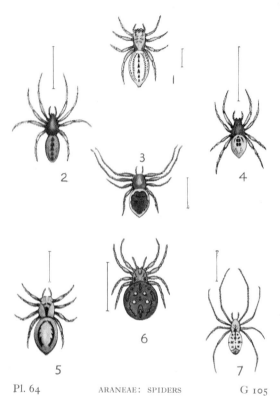

1. *Euophrys frontalis.*   2. *Segestria senoculata.*   3. A Crab Spider, *Diaea dorsata.*   4. *Ciniflo similis.*   5. *Evarcha blancardi.*   6. *Aranea reaumuri.*   7. *Labulla thoracica.*   Pages 112, 114.

a constant companion in man's dwellings. Another is *Fannia canicularis* (Plate **58**, *3*), the Lesser House Fly. *Orthellia cornicina* (Plate **60**, *2*) is another common Green Bottle.

A true parasite lives entirely at the expense of its host. The family Larvaevoridae (Tachinidae) are of this kind, especially prevalent in larvae and pupae of Butterflies and Moths; they also attack Spiders and other Arthropods. Parasitic larvae do not attack vital parts of the host, or they would be unable to complete their own development, but when the time for pupation comes they bring about the host's death. *Larvaevora fera* (Plate **60**, *4*—female) parasitizes larvae of the order Lepidoptera, including the caterpillar of the Large White Butterfly (*Pieris brassicae*) which is a pest of cabbage. Plate **56** shows a Parasitic Fly before and after its wings have developed.

Not all dipterous parasites cause the death of the host, especially when the latter is large, but much distress results from such parasitism. One of the best known of this type of Fly is *Gasterophilus intestinalis* (Plate **60**, *3*—female), the common Horse Bot Fly. Its eggs are licked up by the animal in whose stomach the larvae then develop. The Fly is now often included with the family Muscidae, but it was formerly classed with the Oestridae, an extensive family whose larvae are all internal parasites of large mammals.

There is a group of True Flies, the Pupipara, which have become exclusively external parasites of warm-blooded animals and birds. They exhibit remarkable structural changes of a degenerate kind, the result of their highly specialized parasitical habits. Among the family Hippoboscidae there is *Ornithomya avicularia* (Plate **60**, *5*—female), a common blood-sucking parasite of birds. Some species are entirely devoid of wings, such as *Melophagus ovinus* (Plate **58**, *2*), which lives in the fleece of Sheep. It is known as the Sheep Ked, Sheep Louse or Sheep Tick. The family Nycteribiidae consists of small parasites of Bats. Our largest species, *Nycteribia biarticulata* (Plate **58**, *4*), is very spider-like in appearance, but it has only the six legs of adult insects. The prominent, well-developed claws of these insects are characteristic of parasites which cling to hosts.

The foregoing species (of the group Pupipara, " pupa-bearing ") lay a fully developed larva, which immediately pupates. The family Braulidae, also wingless parasites, lay eggs, and because of this there are objections to including them with the Pupipara. Braulidae are parasites of Bees. *Braula coeca* (Plate **58**, *5*) is the Bee Louse, well known to bee-keepers.

Order APHANIPTERA. *Fleas.*

Description. Small, flat insects, some without eyes. Antennae short and thick. Mouth-parts adapted for piercing and sucking. The adult insects only are parasites of mammals and birds. Metamorphosis complete.

Classification. The order is divided into three distinct families. Also called SIPHONAPTERA. (47 British species.)

The classification of insects followed in this book illustrates the evolutionary progress of insects, and we have seen to what degree of perfection evolution has attained in the last two orders, the HYMENOPTERA and DIPTERA. The comity of insects as arranged by entomologists into scientific groupings is more than a convenience for classification; it permits us, in addition, to appreciate more fully the inter-relationship existing between species. It may show, for instance, how a family specialization has changed in one or more related species. To an enquiring mind this gives rise to interesting speculation, which to produce useful conclusions will need to be stimulated by extensive scientific knowledge—such as that of biochemistry, much of which is, however, still shrouded in mystery.

Aphaniptera, Fleas, have always been a puzzle to the entomologist. They are not closely related to any other order of insects, and no trace of wings can be found in them, yet, unlike primitive insects, they undergo complete metamorphosis—even a cocoon is present. It is therefore most likely that Fleas early in their evolutionary history became specialized parasites. We have seen how in the order Diptera (Flies) certain species (Pupipara) have degenerated in structure through having become specialized parasites. In some respects the present order, the members of which are exclusively parasitic, shows a very distant relationship to Flies.

Fleas live by sucking the blood of mammals and birds, many of them being confined to a particular species. They shun light and are attracted to body-warmth. The Fleas on a dead animal will forsake it on the approach of a warm-blooded creature, which has not necessarily to be its normal host. The Fleas of a rat which has died from plague may leap on to a passing man, thus providing the essentials for transmitting the dreaded disease. The bacillus of bubonic plague is introduced by a complicated method of inoculation (e.g., by scratching bacillus-infected Flea excreta beneath the skin).

Only the adult Flea is a blood-sucker. When eggs are produced they fall off the host on to the ground or floor of the places it frequents. On emergence the larva, which has no eyes or legs, feeds on detritus ; it is not a parasite, so the larva of the Human Flea, *Pulex irritans* (Plate **58**, *6*), is consequently found only in dwellings of unclean people. After undergoing two moults, the larva spins a cocoon, in which it remains for a variable time until stimulated by external vibrations, such as may happen when a person enters a room. Emergence then occurs, and is consequently at a most suitable moment for leaping on to a host.

THE STUDY OF INSECTS

The order Aphaniptera concludes our brief survey of the class Insecta. We have seen how varied in structure and how beautiful in coloration Insects can be ; it is therefore not surprising that men and women of many generations have shown great interest in these small creatures. Indeed, the first records we possess of them are in works of art, but in these the form and coloration are shown only as accessory embellishments of a landscape or some other artistic conception. Eventually, however, the Insects themselves were studied, and it will be seen from the list on page 23 that entomologists have demonstrated the extent and variety to be found in the Insecta. Several of the orders, of course, are of interest only to the scientifically minded, and so great are the numbers of species in the many orders that it is obvious that the beginner will probably wish to devote his interest to one or two of those most commonly to be observed. Good introductory books to most of these orders—books which will at the same time remain of lasting interest—are those included in the " Wayside and Woodland " series (Warne). In these will be found descriptions of all the commoner species of the order dealt with, as well as many less commonly found in the British Isles.

CLASS ARACHNIDA

Order ARANEAE. *Spiders.*

Classification. The order ARANEAE, or Spiders, belongs to the class ARACHNIDA, in which are included such varied Arthropods (phylum *ARTHROPODA*, or jointed-footed animals) as Harvestmen (*OPILIONES*, or *PHALANGIDAE*), False-scorpions (*CHELONETHI*, or *PSEUDOSCORPIONES*), and Mites (*ACARI*), in addition to orders not represented in the British Isles, bringing the total of orders in this class to eleven, one of which is represented only by fossil forms. Different species of Arachnids often bear little resemblance to each other. A Spider and the large foreign fish-like King-crab (*Limulus*)—a living fossil with a direct ancestry of millions of years—have no apparent morphological affinity, and indeed this class serves more than anything else as a convenient way of grouping a strange assortment of creatures.

Description. The differences we notice immediately between Spiders and Insects are the following :—

Spiders	*Insects.*
(*a*) Two divisions of the body, the *cephalothorax*, the head-chest—the head and thorax being fused together—and the *abdomen*.	(*a*) Three divisions of the body, *head*, *thorax* and *abdomen*.
(*b*) Four pairs of legs.	(*b*) Three pairs of legs in adults.
(*c*) No antennae.	(*c*) Almost always with antennae.
(*d*) No wings.	(*d*) Wings usually present.
(*e*) Usually four to eight Simple eyes, never Compound.	(*e*) Imagines (adult insects) often have two kinds of eyes, Compound (multiple-faceted) and Simple (ocelli).

Anatomy. The cephalothorax bears in front a number of simple eyes, their position and arrangement helping in classification. The *chelicerae*, the jaws or fangs, are stout, and contain the poison-glands from which ducts lead near to the tips of the sharp points. There is much difference in structure, according to species. To the cephalothorax are also attached the eight legs and a pair of palpi, or pedipalps (Plate **59**). The palpi are remarkable appendages. In the female they are simple in construction, each ending in a claw (Plate **59**). They help in feeling and compensate for the absence of antennae. In the male the palpi are complicated sex-organs, a male being easily recognizable by the swollen palpi. The female genitalia are situated in the lower surface and at the front of the abdomen, where is the opening of the oviduct. The aperture is called the *epigyne*. The method of pairing is unique in the animal kingdom. The male's testis is at the base of the abdomen; the sperm is deposited by him on a specially constructed platform of silk, or he may dispense with this refinement. He then dips his palpi in the fluid and, thus charged, he transfers it to the female's epigyne for storing in reservoirs, called *spermathecae*, until required when eggs are laid. The sexual act is fraught with dangers for the male, as he is smaller than his mate, who will attack him and make a wedding breakfast of him, but often his smaller size and greater agility will save him.

Spiders are, like insects, creatures guided by instinct. The persistent energy of insects would appear in Spiders to be replaced by patience, which the scientist would no doubt prefer to term periods of inertia between immediate responses to external stimuli. At least that is so in respect of numerous species which lie in wait for victims; it does not at first appear quite so obvious in those which maraud in search of prey.

Spiders are fierce denizens of the undergrowth jungle. Many of their kind have invaded our houses, and even a strange unsuitable element, water, on the surface of which they carry on their relentless hunting. One, *Argyroneta aquatica* (Plate **62**, *5*), the Water Spider, even goes into the water itself and lives there. They are always in pursuit of living prey, usually insects, so that Spiders are praised because they are most active insect destroyers. It is pointed out that as every meal they make means the slaughter of a live and mostly pestilential creature, it follows that their activities are useful to man and the plants on which he depends for his existence. We are told to remember the old saying—

> If you wish to live and thrive,
> Let the spider run alive.

However, the zoologist will remark that this is counterbalanced by the fact that Spiders attack all insects. They cannot be expected to discriminate conveniently for us between the allies and enemies of man, and the most that can be said in their favour is that they reduce the numbers of *all* insects. Spiders are actually of no economic importance. They neither harm man's possessions nor do they contribute in their activities anything of great value. Attempts have been made, it is true, to utilize the silk of Spiders, but it is evident from experiments that on technical or economic grounds no industry could ever be created to rival in any way that which has been built up on the cocoon-spinning activities of Silkworms (larvae of Silk Moths). Spiders are unique in their dependence on silk. It is used for making snares, for tying up victims whose struggles are likely to prove troublesome, for travelling—and even for " flying ", as well as for the cocoons to protect the eggs.

The female is an adept at finding suitable sites to lay her eggs, round which she then spins a protective mantle of silk. Some even go further than this : *Pisaura listeri* (Plates **59** and **61** ; Plate **62**, *4*), a Hunting Spider, carries her cocoon about with her, so does the Wolf Spider *Lycosa*, a rather sombre-coloured Spider, though she goes one better to attract attention to her ways, for whilst she is hunting the young cling to her back.

Species that carry their cocoon about with them do so by having it attached to the jaws, or to the spinnerets. The spinnerets are the openings in the abdomen from which the silk emerges. The Spider will offer violent resistance if we try to detach her precious possession. Smell seems to be the thing that attracts her to the cocoon, because if we take it away from her, and rub it on some light pellet, she will take this new object and carry it away, but not for long, as she soon becomes aware of the trickery and will start seeking her rightful property. Another mother will be found tearing her cocoon open to allow her offspring to escape. These species are thus doing their best in our eyes to retrieve the appalling reputation with which their kind is reproached.

Normally parental care ceases with the spinning of the cocoon ; some do not even go so far. If the female comes across her young she will not hesitate to make a meal of them. E. A. Robins, a well-known arachnologist, found that the young of *Ciniflo similis* (Plate **64**, *4*) were actually eating their mother, who was still alive ; experiments were repeated annually " so it was not casual observance ", as it happened again and again. This Spider is the commonest and most wide-spread in these islands, and is usually found in cellars, sheds and the like. It is also one of our largest species, measuring 13 mm. ($\frac{1}{2}$ in.) long.

The number of eggs laid by Spiders is often in the neighbourhood of eight hundred, the large number being required because the newly hatched Spiderlings do not feed until after the first moult : life begins in a very earnest manner indeed inside the silken home, for cannibalism breaks out, and it has been estimated that only about one hundred young Spiders finally emerge.

When this happens they are miniatures of their parents. There is nothing that corresponds to the larval and pupal stages of insects. On the breaking of the cocoon the young are bent on dispersal, which some species effect by climbing on a fence, or other exposed position, and letting out strands of silk, or gossamer as it is called, in the breeze. When the Spiderling finds that the wind gives sufficient pull it lets go, and so we have the remarkable feat of a flightless creature sailing through the air. Some observers maintain that Spiders are able to control the length of gossamer, paying out more silk when the wind falls, and " shortening sail " when it increases. They naturally have to go where the wind takes them, often to an early doom. A classical example of this was furnished by Darwin, who in 1832, whilst on the *Beagle*, observed that the rigging of the vessel was suddenly invaded by numerous gossamer-borne Spiders. The *Beagle* was some sixty miles from the nearest land. Since then cases have been recorded of much longer flights.

Most Spiders do not spin webs, though they all make use of silk. When webs are made they differ according to the species of Spider. The commonest House Spider, *Tegenaria domestica* (Plate **62**, *2*), makes the familiar untidy maze, whilst our large Garden Spider, *Aranea diadema*

(Plate **62**, *3*) and *A. reaumuri* (Plate **64**, *6*), are makers of complex and beautiful webs. The Spiders often vary in colour, especially the latter species.

Other common spiders are *Segestria senoculata* (Plate **64**, *2*), which is widely distributed; it is often found wandering on walls, but these are more particularly the haunt of *Salticus scenicus* (Plate **62**, *1*), the little Zebra Spider. *Diaea dorsata* (Plate **64**, *3*), common in the South but not in the North, is one of our most beautiful species. It belongs to the family of Thomisidae, known as the Crab Spiders, as does *Misumena calycina* (Plate **62**, *6*); the popular family name refers to the fact that they can run forwards, backwards or sideways. They do not spin webs, but lie in wait among vegetation, or in flowers, where they seize their victims. *M. calycina* even attacks Bees; the Spider may often be found when a Bee is not seen to move away from a flower, which normally it leaves after a few seconds. It will be found held in the Spider's fangs. Protective coloration, very evident in these spiders, is shown in one of the genus *Philodromus* (Plate **61**); it is on a tree trunk, at rest over its cocoon.

Evarcha blancardi (Plate **64**, *5*) is very common everywhere, as also is *Euophrys frontalis* (Plate **64**, *1*). Common in cellars, and in rooms at night is *Labulla thoracica* (Plate **64**, *7*). It has quite handsome markings. Another species common in houses is *Tegenaria atrica* (Plate **63**). On the same plate is shown the photograph of a captive outdoor species, *Micrommata viridissima* (Plate **63**); it is a male, as shown by the abdomen. The female is entirely green.

INDEX

115

116

117

124

Printed in Great Britain by Richard Clay (The Chaucer Press), Ltd.,
Bungay, Suffolk
858.1168